Shedding the Chrysalis

NAVIGATING CAREERS IN HIGHER EDUCATION

The success of faculty in higher education is shaped by varying factors at both the individual and institutional levels. The Navigating Careers in Higher Education series seeks to examine and understand how faculty members and administrators navigate careers and their aspirations to succeed. The series will include books that adopt an interdisciplinary, scholarly approach as well as personal testimonies of individuals sharing their own lived experiences, including challenges faced and lessons learned. With a US or global focus, topics include the role of higher education institutions; the effects of growing nontenure-track faculty; the challenge of research agenda that may be perceived as controversial; maintaining a life-work balance; and entering leadership positions.

SERIES EDITOR

Mangala Subramaniam, Senior Vice Provost for Faculty Affairs
Virginia Commonwealth University

SERIES COEDITOR

M. Cristina Alcalde, Vice President for Institutional Diversity and Inclusion
Miami University

OTHER TITLES IN THIS SERIES

Higher Education Careers Beyond the Professoriate
Karen Cardozo, Katherine Kearns, and Shannan Palma (Eds.)

The Challenges of Minoritized Contingent Faculty in Higher Education
Edna Chun and Alvin Evans

Transforming Leadership Pathways for Humanities Professionals in Higher Education
Roze Hentschell and Catherine E. Thomas (Eds.)

*Dismantling Institutional Whiteness:
Emerging Forms of Leadership in Higher Education*
M. Cristina Alcalde and Mangala Subramaniam (Eds.)

Shedding the Chrysalis

Black Women Leading in Higher Education

Edited by Olga M. Welch and Carolyn R. Hodges

Purdue University Press, West Lafayette, Indiana

Cataloging-in-Publication Data is available from the Library of Congress.
978-1-62671-138-9 (hardback)
978-1-62671-139-6 (paperback)
978-1-62671-140-2 (epub)
978-1-62671-141-9 (epdf)

Cover: Rose butterfly (ornithoptera priamus): johnandersonphoto/iStock via Getty Images Plus. Monarch Emerges: gprentice/iStock via Getty Images Plus.

CONTENTS

From the Chrysalis to the Long Green Table

Afterword

ACKNOWLEDGMENTS

We offer our sincere gratitude to the wonderful colleagues who were a part of our journey in putting together this volume. Our contributors, comprising a variety of seasoned and promising aspirational Black women leaders in higher education, shared triumphant experiences, challenges, and exemplary perspectives we think will provide inspiration to other minoritized women following that path.

Sincere thanks are also due to Cristina Alcalde, Vice President for Institutional Diversity and Inclusion, Miami University, and Mangala Subramaniam, Senior Vice Provost for Faculty Affairs, Virginia Commonwealth University, whose series on Navigating Careers in Higher Education at Purdue University Press has been an inspiration and guide for work we have pursued for several years.

We are deeply indebted to our families—our husbands, children, and their families—who supported our work, and especially to our mothers and grandmothers who came before us as models for strong leadership built on hard work, unwavering dedication, and integrity.

We, as coeditors coming from different academic backgrounds and leadership experiences, celebrate a long-term professional relationship that has stimulated us to interrogate leadership in higher education through different lenses and research projects we developed across disciplinary lines. Through a long-term collegial bond built on mutual trust, abiding support, and good humor, we have taken advantage of our shared philosophy on the importance of developing mentoring relationships to advance the careers of others whom we have guided, and by whose experiences we also have been enlightened.

Olga M. Welch and Carolyn R. Hodges

INTRODUCTION

Voices of Black Women from the Contested Terrain of Higher Education Leadership

OLGA M. WELCH AND CAROLYN R. HODGES

T his book is for everyone. We are writing for people of all races and ethnicities, gender identities and sexual orientations, physical abilities, and ages, as we all have a large responsibility for bringing attention to and addressing systemic inequities in academic leadership. We chose to situate our argument with a focus on Black women leaders who have been challenged by and have witnessed racial injustices in academic leadership and to highlight them from various levels of experience at a variety of stages. In *Stamped from the Beginning: The Definitive History of Racist Ideas in America*, Kendi opens his chronicle of the history of racist thought and practice in America with Jefferson Davis's declaration in 1860 that the "'inequality of the Black and white races' was 'stamped from the beginning'" (3). We are all, in fact, stamped by racism and the collective inequities that established the United States. We contend that all oppressions interlock, and whether individuals experience it directly, as did indigenous peoples, African Americans, Mexican Americans, and Asian Americans; whether they struggle to legislate against the painful legacy of their forebears; or whether they are engaged in perpetuating that legacy, both the oppressed and the oppressors inevitably suffer the consequences at some level.

In answer to those who insist that they are not responsible for the ills their ancestors inflicted on marginalized groups and therefore dismiss any obligation to resolve the resulting harms that continue to disempower those striving for inclusion and equity, we would argue that because our nation was founded on the systemic nature of oppression, this book is about everyone's interconnected history and the duty of all of us to dismantle a system that enslaves everyone. Only then can we begin to move toward the more perfect union proclaimed in our Constitution and long anticipated and dreamed of by our collective ancestors. Whatever your belief systems, wherever your religious or non-religious affiliations lie, whatever your race or ethnicity and how you define it, and whether you identify as gay or straight, questioning or non-binary, marginalized or majority, we are all stamped by the collective inequities that framed our country's origin. That is not woke; that's a fact.

At the same time, we are writing to highlight and encourage experienced and emerging Black women leaders in higher education. Too often they tend to be buried under other broad categories, for example, women of color, women in nontraditional roles, all women, and all people of color, which can have the effect of obscuring unique aspects of their experiences. We do not want to speak for the experiences of other marginalized groups in the academy but seek to provide voices of Black women as an illustrative model for others who have been excluded in their efforts to assume and conduct leadership roles.

This book is for everyone, because we assert that anti-Blackness is a foundation upon which, over centuries, many forms of discrimination have been built. The Black feminist lens that underlies the chapters in this book stands as a reminder of the interlocking oppressions that compel many to unite and mobilize against racial, ethnic, gender, and class disparities in society that are in many aspects mirrored in practices and processes in higher education. George Lipsitz alludes to those interlocking oppressions in the twentieth-anniversary edition of his compelling work, *The Possessive Investment in Whiteness: How White People Profit* *from Identity Politics,* wherein his reflections on the longstanding crisis we face regarding race in conflict with possessive whiteness draw attention to contemporary social movements that are grounded not just exclusively in race but in the interconnected oppressions. He asserts that the movements, which are

> often race based but rarely race bound. . . . see racism as innately intersectional, as *ever* present but *never* present in isolation from sexism, homophobia, imperial conquest, and class subordination. These movements acknowledge the long fetch of history, the depressing collective, cumulative, and continuing consequences of slavery unwilling to die, yet they also perceive new possibilities for the present and for the future. (viii)

Finally, **this book is for everyone** because the contributors' experiences and ideas serve as a motivation and ideally a resource for any leader with serious wishes to disrupt the long-standing status quo in institutional leadership and to address the gaps in diverse representation and inclusion. Their journeys are important for current and emerging minoritized leaders committed to establishing and sustaining an equitable leadership domain.

Current challenges and threats against diversity and inclusion as well as increasingly robust resistance to teaching the history of racism and its lingering impact make it imperative to highlight those topics as they relate to higher education in general and to institutional leadership in particular. Recently, a more intense gaze has been directed on women of color in higher education who, in their ascendance to and journey as leaders, are forced to grapple with aspects of power and resistance, systemic obstacles grounded in possessive investment in whiteness, and long-standing policies and practices deemed to be inviolable.

A growing body of literature engaging in this conversation uses an autoethnographic framework built on personal narratives, qualitative research, and the concept of intersectionality which describes the ways in which women of color in academia are marginalized by race, gender, and class. In their volume *Presumed Incompetent II: Race, Class, Power, and Resistance of Women in Academia*, editors Yolanda Flores Niemann, Gabriella Gutiérrez y Muhs, and Carmen G. González feature women of color in the academy who display the variety of ways in which they have encountered and resisted the effects of race, class, and power dynamics that have threatened to diminish or erase their presence and impact. This compilation of thirty-two chapters covers a variety of issues in sections covering tenure and promotion; academic leadership; social class; bullying, white fragility, and microaggressions; activism, resistance, and public engagement. The volume follows the positive reception of a preceding anthology edited by Gabriella Gutiérrez y Muhs, Yolanda Flores Nieman, Carmen G, Gonzales, and Angela Harris, *Presumed Incompetent: The Intersections of Race and Class for Women in Academia*, where discussions of general campus climate, faculty-student relationships, network of allies, social class in academia, and the tenure and promotion process combine to illustrate the theme of inimical presumed incompetence that plagues and at times stymies the academic careers of women of color.

A compilation edited by Antija M. Allen and Justin Stewart, *We're Not OK: Black Faculty Experiences and Higher Education Strategies*, specifically touts its use of an autoethnographic framework in a series of essays illuminating the experiences of Black faculty and highlighting several of the structural deterrents that have impeded efforts to demonstrate commitment to diversity and inclusion, in particular at predominantly white postsecondary institutions (PWIs). While their primary focus is Black faculty and leadership is not singled out as a major topic, they do address student experiences (undergraduate and graduate) and cover a wide array of significant issues in three major sections: (1) The Journey from Student to Faculty, (2) Promoting Mental Wellness, and (3) Strategies for Inclusion and Retention, featuring selected programs of promise.

In *Dismantling Institutional Whiteness: Emerging Forms of Leadership in Higher Education*, M. Cristina Alcalde and Mangala Subramaniam feature women of color in leadership roles in higher education through engrossing personal narratives that recount the systemic biases and structural oppressions grounded in whiteness that impede success; their compelling stories, analyses, and lessons learned are also meant to be an impetus for change. Hodges and Welch contributed to the work a chapter that built upon and expanded ideas in their previous work on academic leadership, *Truth Without Tears: African American Women Deans Share Lessons in Leadership*, where the focal points rested specifically on their experiences as deans who were "firsts" (Black and women) in the positions at their respective PWIs.

All of these books are significant antecedents to the narrower, more pointed direction of this volume, featuring Black women serving in or on the path to be a part of higher education administration, and we present their voices as an inspiration to other minoritized populations to share their unique experiences. It is critically important to bring voices from the margins to the center of the dialogue on what it means to engage in the practice of leadership. In asserting this, we maintain that the center has been too narrow in its gaze, relying as it does almost exclusively on the perspectives of dominant elites while obscuring or even obfuscating the lived experiences of those who have been relegated to the margins as higher education leaders. As Sarah Ahmed points out in her important work, *On Being Included: Racism and Diversity in Institutional Life*, "feminism of color provides us with a ways of thinking through power in terms of 'intersectionality,' to think about and through the points at which power relations meet" (14).

Thus, this book is a call to action for institutional leaders to address areas for change in the narrative surrounding academic leadership in ways that reimagine that role as an inclusive space that enables and authentically supports the full participation of those who traditionally have been minoritized and, as a result, less than fully engaged in their work.

We hold that unless higher education widens the discourse on what it means to enact the role of leader, it will not be able to continue the process of broadening academic leadership in ways that are meaningful and sustainable. At the risk of appropriating an overused axiom, we submit that those who do not learn from a failed history are doomed to repeat it, and the glaring threats within the structure that uphold that failed history will remain as barriers to positive change.

MINDING THE GAP

Although the number of Black women who have shattered the glass ceiling and risen to key leadership roles in higher education at PWIs has slowly begun to rise, the disparity between their representation in numbers and that of white men and women remains wide, with reports showing Black women with lowest percentages after white men, white women, and Black men, in that order (Silbert et al.; Chance; Davis and Maldonado; McConner). The increase in Black women administrators reflects their growth in numbers in attaining doctoral degrees, achieving tenure, progressing to full professor status, and achieving national and international recognition for their professional achievements. Of course, the simple fact of their gradually growing presence in leadership positions does not address the disparity between their presence and that of their white colleagues, nor does it offer an appraisal of challenges faced in their roles as administrators, their professional development in the positions, or the impact of their presence on transforming the vision of leadership.

Recent studies suggest that this slow rise in their mobility is not only about the shortage of Black women prepared to assume those executive-level positions but that it is also about how their lived experiences in those roles reflect institutional responses to them as a new face of leadership and unveil a disassociation between the institutions' expressed commitment to diversity and inclusion and actual practice and implementation. Thus, despite the growing numbers of Black women earning doctorates and entering higher education, systemic inequities fueled by gender and racial power adversely affect the possibility of sustained increases in their presence at the highest levels of academic administration. A 2022 study jointly published by the Women's Power Gap Initiative of the Eos Foundation and the American Association of University Women that looked at elite research universities in the United States (Carnegie Classification high research) reports that "Women, particularly women of color, are underrepresented among all leadership positions, both internally and on university boards. Their highest proportions are in the president's cabinets (net of academic deans), but that is rarely a pathway position to the presidency. On the other side, women comprise only one in ten system presidents, and there are no women of color at this level" (Silbert et al. 12).

The conundrum that Black women face raises the following questions for study: What is the connection across the concepts of power, title, and leadership and the role of race and gender in navigating the administrative terrain? In what ways are the roles of diversity, equity, and inclusion contextualized by those in power who define the leadership position? What impact does that contextualization have on the sense of purpose and meaning for Black women with experience as well as for their promising and talented peers aspiring to leadership roles? How might Black women leaders and their white counterparts reimagine the role of leadership and create a system that addresses the existing gaps, not only for those currently serving in those roles but also for emerging leaders who often are left out of the discussion?

EXAMINING POWER AND THE STRUCTURAL NATURE OF RACIAL BARRIERS

In a study addressing the underrepresentation of women in leadership roles in corporations, Michelle Ryan and Alexander Haslam note that once women seemingly have shattered the glass ceiling, they find themselves precariously situated on a glass cliff. Pointing to the circumstances of the appointment of these women that result in reports of inferior performance or failure, they argue that men often place women in roles "associated with an increased risk of negative consequences" (83), thus elevating them to an insecure position described as a glass cliff that all too often leads to failure. In a later study, Kelly Oakes adds that the potential for failure on the glass cliff is more likely to affect people in a variety of ethnic groups who traditionally have been underrepresented in leadership roles.

Placement of women amid a crisis is important to consider as a factor for problems they face when they accede to executive-level positions, but for Black women it is not likely the single reason for difficulties, for the impact of dealing with internal problems within the organization is heightened by a combination of other factors. In the haste to be seen as making a substantial effort at addressing lack of diversity, institutional leaders at PWIs often welcome Black women, many of whom are the first Black individuals at their institution in upper-level administration, into leadership roles in units fraught with crises, but very often those women are held back from enacting their full power in those roles. Their difficulties rendered by the power gap, in turn, can affect placement of future Black women as institutional leaders.

BEING VS. DOING: REIMAGINING EDUCATIONAL LEADERSHIP

Studies mentioned above that analyze testimonies from women of color also suggest that those examples are less about the internal problems that need to be addressed than they are about how the institutional leaders regard and interact with them; furthermore, those leaders to whom the women report often declare their commitment to diversity even as their actions result in their simply guarding the status quo. In a sense, whether intentional or not, their decisions allow them to have it both ways, that is, to appear to be embracing diversity and inclusion in leadership roles while simultaneously offloading troubling racial and social justice issues and crises onto those placed in the positions. This, in turn, creates scenarios likely to discourage the ambitions of other emerging leaders or to give them a skewed understanding of what it takes to succeed.

Once they occupy a high-profile position, many Black women recognize not only that they do not have the promised or expected support but also that, in attempting to move forward with the duties and goals with which they have been charged, they face adversity on personal and professional levels from careerist academic leaders who want to "be" leaders, that is, bear the title of the role but are not "doing" the job of leadership and instead are relying on performative interactions. In *The Ego is the Enemy* Ryan Holiday warns against allowing the ego to replace ethics—to become, as he posits, the enemy—when he claims, "It's about the doing, not the recognition. Easier in the sense that you don't need to compromise. Harder because each opportunity ... must be evaluated along strict guidelines ..." (34). Performative leaders are much more interested in playing and replaying the narrative in their own minds as confirmation of their superiority in order to prove their innate ability to know what is needed even as they too often fail to enact the responsibilities of the role.

The ego, then, becomes the enemy when one uses those narratives to engage in actions and behaviors that are less about the goals of the institution, or the department, or whatever the context in which one is a leader, and more about burnishing one's credentials, validating one's own narrative about the brilliance of one's unique approach to leadership, and convincing others that that narrative is tantamount to visionary stewardship. As a result, Black women can find that such leaders exclude them from discourses and decision-making related to their jobs in ways that question their legitimacy and competence and hamper their efforts. For us, "doing" the job of leadership is an enterprise that involves everyone and must engage everyone.

Academic hierarchy is a hotly contested terrain of leadership. Once led exclusively by white men, that terrain, in response to charges of sexism, has exhibited some progress in broadening its diversity, but the shattering of the glass ceiling opened opportunities for many white women while leaving Black women lagging in attaining those positions or, when they do move forward, finding themselves on a dangerously slick cliff. Furthermore, we must recognize that this embattled terrain exists at every level in academia and is rooted in systemic inequities that are magnified when examined through the lens of intersectionality. The concept of intersectionality in some ways has raised even more questions in the academy as institutional leaders are compelled to respond to calls for equity and inclusion from a host of minoritized groups who are excluded not only based on race, ethnicity, and class but also on ableism, sexual orientation, and gender identity, and many PWIs struggle to commit to effect change in the face of internal and external resistance.

In order to implement transformative change, we must ask ourselves continually what approaches might be employed and how Black women can engage with those around them in the academy to make meaningful and sustainable adjustments that move beyond tolerance and a politics of civility (Zamalin) to policies and practices that have the power to deconstruct the status quo and offer a new push for the ongoing enterprise of addressing racial and social justice. All minoritized groups within academic hierarchies are like butterflies emerging from a chrysalis. Black women leaders experience that emergence as if wrapped in a crucible whose material is a hardened and overlaid composition of racism, sexism, and homophobia leading to marginalization within an exclusionary system that has built up over time. This phenomenon regrettably has become all too prominent in many aspects of our daily lives and is driven by political, religious, and social allegiances that threaten to destroy our communal obligations to one another. Thus, in higher education, we all must be aware of and digest these experiences if we are to alter the anachronistic narratives and approaches surrounding higher education leadership, while we take on the challenges to find ways to create a terrain that is not driven by cultural divisions and personal agendas but is instead led by a firm and steady foundation supporting diversity, equity, and inclusion.

OVERVIEW OF THE BOOK

The book features, along with our introduction, additional chapter, and an afterword, the voices of experienced and emerging Black women in a variety of academic leadership roles at PWIs ranging from the level of postdoctoral research fellow up to positions reporting to central administration. In focusing on Black women leaders at PWIs, we do so because very often they are the very first in these leadership positions and in many cases have few, if any, Black colleagues at their level in other units. Therefore, they are under more intense scrutiny and often are misrepresented and mischaracterized in terms of their enacting the role and making decisions on a daily basis. We are well aware that Black women leaders occupy those positions in other institutional contexts, most notably, HBCUs. However, in our case, we and the contributors to this volume speak to the experiences that we have had at PWIs because that is our context and because programs focusing on diversity, equity, and inclusion originate and are implemented within those academic institutions, presumably to exemplify diversity goals outlined in their strategic vision and provide evidence of an inviting campus culture.

We centered our work on Black women and their multiple identities in order to: (a) include the vision of others whose journeys have connections with and build upon what we as coeditors have written about our personal experiences as deans (Hodges and Welch); (b) provide a Black feminist perspective that highlights what their journeys reveal about the need to address "racial realism" (Bell) within higher education administration; (c) call attention to a variety of levels in academic hierarchy to emphasize the continuum across the lived experiences of these women, some of whom have served in multiple upper-level administrative roles; and (d) underscore what these women have learned from mentors and allies as well as adversaries that can help us to imagine and perhaps build a different, more stable domain in leadership for a variety of minoritized groups.

In "Conquering the Glass Cliff and Riding Deceptive Escalators: Black Women Leading with and beyond Difference" Welch and Hodges examine those deceptive elevators to the top that have failed to address the disparities in numbers between Black women and their white counterparts in key leadership roles in higher education. The chapter features (a) the trope of the chrysalis and the crucible of race; (b) the phenomenon of weathering caused by structural racism and its effect on the health and welfare of Black women (Villarosa); (c) the relevance of Heather McGhee's vision of the web of mutuality, an essential mindset for addressing the cultural divide that enhances weathering and impedes the goal of minding the gap. The chapter proposes concepts to consider in reimagining institutional leadership as an inclusive space that is critical to enabling the fully authentic participation of Black women administrators in the academy.

In "The DEI Conundrum for Black Women Leaders" Stephanie Rowley discusses how reflection on the watershed moments of the George Floyd and Breanna Taylor murders and the COVID-19 pandemic bear the potential to ignite change in higher education. She offers a thoughtful consideration of the connections between those moments and the precarious state of leadership defined by the concept of the glass cliff and addresses the tension between the critical DEI skills that Black women have honed by necessity, including the expectation that they serve in a "mammy" role to nurture those who have been marginalized and deliver healing where trust has been broken.

Wanda Blanchett examines both historical and recent data to illustrate the state of Black women in academic leadership, in general, and specifically at top research universities in her chapter "The Reason Universities Don't Have More Black Women in Higher Education Academic Leadership Is Because They Don't Want Them! Revisiting the Past to Reshape the Present." She explores some of the challenges Black women experience in navigating the Ivory Tower as faculty on their journey to becoming academic administrators and offers suggestions on how we might reimagine higher education leadership to more fully respect, embrace, and make use of the tremendous talents and leadership Black women bring to the academy.

Postdoctoral research fellow Tam'ra K. Francis turns our attention to how the onset of the triple pandemic highlighted the contradiction between the current operating model of academic leadership and the goals of equity-seeking organizations in her chapter "From Gatekeeping to Groundskeeping: Cultivating Seeds of Black Women Emerging Leaders." She singles out two concurrent trends: an increased reliance on Black scholars to provide DEI-related guidance and the Great Resignation of Black scholars at all academic levels. Additionally, she deliberates the problematic rise and effects of recent legislative backlashes aimed at academic freedom and diversity efforts in higher education. For her, these shifts raise questions for institutional leadership surrounding trauma-informed care and support for Black scholars' academic development during trying times.

Drawing from her role as an administrator at an institution for deaf and hard of hearing students and her work as a certified cultural diversity professional, Janice D. M. Mitchell explores the role cultural dimensions play in achieving leadership positions in PWIs in "Intercultural Dimensions and Higher Education Leadership: Barriers and Stepping Stones for Black Women Professionals in Unique Predominantly White Institutions." She points out that Black women who find themselves teaching and leading on the defense must tackle hurdles that are often determined by *cultural mindsets* guided by assumptions about race and gender. Mitchell identifies three specific types of cultural mindsets as they affect estimations of overall competencies; evaluations of diversity and inclusion; and connections between professional competence, allyship, and ageism. She reflects on how the assumptions embedded in those mindsets can be strictly exported onto Black women seeking academic recognition and support and can cast them in a cloud of *competence invisibility*.

In "From the Chrysalis to the Long Green Table" Olga Welch offers closing thoughts on the monumental challenges of leadership, followed by "They Wouldn't Let Us Lead . . .," an afterword by Carol Camp Yeakey, a distinguished university educator, scholar, and leader, who offers reflections on how the struggles, disappointments, and triumphs related in the chapters serve as a call and, we hope, an impetus for building models of leadership in higher education that foster diversity and inclusion.

In sum, the contributors' testimonies and reflections underscore what they have learned from mentors and allies as well as from adversaries that can help us to imagine and perhaps build a different, more stable terrain for a variety of diverse leaders in higher education. We have not provided prescriptive stratagems that proffer a "one size fits all" solution for approaching the dilemma of Black women leaders, as each model for change must address the specific institutional context. What is common to them all, however, is the call to build intentionality within transformative institutional governance in order to construct sustainable change and support for inclusive leadership at all levels.

WORKS CITED

Ahmed, Sarah. *On Being Included: Racism and Diversity in Institutional Life.* Duke UP, 2012.

Alcalde, M. Cristina, and Mangala Subramaniam, editors. *Dismantling Institutional Whiteness: Emerging Forms of Leadership in Higher Education.* Purdue UP, 2023.

Allen, Antija M., and Justin T. Stewart, editors. *We're Not OK: Black Faculty Experiences and Higher Education Strategies*. Cambridge UP, 2022.

Bell, Derrick. *Faces at the Bottom of the Well: The Permanence of Racism*. Basic Books, 1992.

Chance, Nuchelle. "Resilient Leadership: A Phenomenological Exploration into How Black Women in Higher Education Leadership Navigate Cultural Adversity." *Journal of Humanistic Psychology*, vol. 62, no. 1, 2022, pp. 44–78. Sage Journals, https://doi.org/10.1177/0021678211003000.

Davis, Deanna R., and Cecilia Maldonado. "Shattering the Glass Ceiling: The Leadership Development of African American Women in Higher Education." *Advancing Women in Leadership*, vol. 35, 2015, pp. 48–64. https://doi.org/10.21423/awlj-v35.a125.

Gutiérrez y Muhs, Gabriella, et al., editors. *Presumed Incompetent: The Intersections of Race and Class for Women in Academia*. Utah State UP, 2012.

Hodges, Carolyn R., and Olga M. Welch. *Truth Without Tears: African American Women Deans Share Lessons in Leadership*. Harvard Education Press, 2018.

Holiday, Ryan. *Ego is the Enemy*. Portfolio / Penguin, 2016.

Kendi, Ibram X. *Stamped from the Beginning: The Definitive History of Racist Ideas in America*. Nation Books, 2022.

Lipsitz, George. Preface. *The Possessive Investment in Whiteness: How White People Profit From Identity Politics*. Twentieth Anniversary ed., Temple UP, 2018.

McConner, Mary. "Black Women in Leadership: An Assessment of the Gender Inequality and Racism That Exists Among Black Women Leaders in Higher Education." *Journal of Higher Education Management*, vol. 29, no. 1, 2014, pp. 78–87.

McGhee, Heather. *The Sum of Us: What Racism Costs Everyone and How We Can Prosper Together*. One World, 2012.

Niemann, Yolanda Flores, et al., editors. *Presumed Incompetent II: Race, Class, and Resistance of Women in Academia*. Utah State UP, 2020.

Oakes, Kelly. "The Invisible Danger of the Glass Cliff." *BBC News Daily* Feb.

2022. https://www.bbc.com/future/article/20220204-the-danger-of-the
-glass-cliff- for-women-and-people-of-colour.

Ryan, Michelle K., and S. Alexander Haslam. "The Glass Cliff: Evidence that
Women are Over- Represented in Precarious Leadership Positions." *British Journal of Management*, vol. 16, no. 2, June 2005, pp. 81–90. Wiley Online Library, https://doi.org/10.1111/j.1467-8551.2005.00433.x.

Silbert, Andrea, et al. "The Women's Power Gap at Elite Universities: Scaling the Ivory Tower. 2022 Study." *The Women's Power Gap Study Series*, Eos Foundation, Jan. 2022, https://www.aauw.org/app/uploads/2022/01/WPG-Power-Gap-at-Elite-Universities-Full-Report.pdf.

Villarosa, Linda. *Under the Skin: The Hidden Toll of Racism on American Lives and on the Health of Our Nation*. Doubleday, 2022.

Zamalin, Alex. *Against Civility: The Hidden Racism in Our Obsession with Civility*. Beacon Press, 2021.

1

CONQUERING THE GLASS CLIFF AND RIDING DECEPTIVE ESCALATORS

Black Women Leading with and beyond Difference

OLGA M. WELCH AND CAROLYN R. HODGES

We delight in the beauty of the butterfly, but rarely admit the changes it has gone through to achieve that beauty.
—MAYA ANGELOU, *POCKET MAYA ANGELOU WISDOM*

We are gods in the chrysalis.
—ELBERT HUBBARD, *THE NOTE BOOK OF ELBERT HUBBARD*

For ages, humankind has been captivated by the butterfly, whose majestic beauty unfolds as part of a complex and complete metamorphosis culminating in a relatively short life cycle. While we are mesmerized by the butterfly's radiant beauty, we tend to minimize or, in many cases, are not fully aware of the intricate process whereby the egg of the adult butterfly becomes a caterpillar, which eventually encases itself in a pupa, or chrysalis, and several weeks later emerges as the adult butterfly. Forces acting on the caterpillar are natural changes, including a complete breakdown and rebuilding on a cellular level to which the insect responds by instinct (American Museum of Natural History).

For us, the butterfly's formative process of evolving within the chrysalis provides a striking analogy for the experience of many Black women leaders in higher education at predominantly white institutions (PWIs). The complex biological process in the butterfly's metamorphosis is a naturally occurring one, involving a miraculous transformation of its form; depending on the impact of the surrounding and uncontrollable forces within nature, all butterflies will not survive through the chrysalis stage. Experienced and emerging Black women "in the chrysalis," as it were, undergo a socializing process that not only determines if and how they emerge as leaders but also plays a significant role in how they manage their journey as leaders. As with the butterfly, all Black women leaders do not survive in the process, either not achieving the desired leadership status or undergoing a disheartening or failed attempt at displaying their talents. Successful or not, their fate is less about the leader who emerges than it is about the impact of their surroundings and the complicated, layered process in which they are immersed and must transform, a process in which restrictions based on racial prejudices and systemic obstacles obstruct their efforts to fulfill the expectations of their administrative roles.

In using this metaphor, we are not engaging in hyperbole but, rather, in fact. For that reason, it is important to consider not only the external social forces that shape their transition to leadership but also, and perhaps more importantly, to acknowledge the significant impact of the legacy of their African heritage as well as the history of slavery in the United States and its persistent aftermath. These women are products of their lived experiences as well as a collective legacy from enslaved ancestors who were forced through a door of no return and taken to a land where they had to forge new lives and learn to understand how to endure pain while finding solace and some level of beauty in the creation of a new life that was not of their choosing. For us, then, the chrysalis is the story; it represents the struggle that produces the delicate, stunning, fragile butterfly in nature as well as the "iron butterfly" encapsulated in successful leadership by Black women.

At every level in higher education Black women have the potential to lead, but many never emerge or have short-lived roles because of the experiences that undermine them. For the butterfly, the chrysalis is meant to serve as a protective shell, but for Black women leading at PWIs the protective chrysalis might be more accurately conceptualized as a fiery crucible, in which unnatural human forces and outdated, exclusionary social conventions are the sources of barriers that threaten to impede and, in some cases, destroy a fruitful transformation, especially for those who are the first Black people in their position and the only Black individuals among their peers in leadership roles. The crucible, then, is race—paradoxically, a nonexistent yet ever present reality. Nearly one hundred years after W. E. B. Du Bois made his prophetic claim in 1903 in *The Souls of Black Folk* about the color line as the problem of the twentieth century, Derek Bell highlighted the persistence of the problem in his *Faces at the Bottom of the Well*, where he extends the message, claiming that "racism in America is not a curable aberration" (x).

Little has changed in the last thirty years to challenge Bell's assessment of the permanence of racism in America. The adversities that engulfed those ancestral iron butterflies and their legacy of strength do not end where the butterfly emerges in the form of the contemporary Black woman leader in higher education. Like their ancestors, Black women in leadership roles continue to be bombarded by often unseen but clearly present and powerful forces of racism, sexism, and compounded effects of intersectionality that cause some to falter in their roles or to leave because of experiences that drive them away and, for many, become the source of lasting trauma. Both those who fail in their endeavors and those who are successful in breaking the proverbial glass ceiling very often undergo the phenomenon of "weathering" that is driven by a racial climate built on exclusion, stereotyping, and devaluation.

WEATHERING AND THE FAILED PROMISE

Public health researcher Arline Geronimus coined the term "weathering" when she started looking at the idea that something about the lived experience of being Black in America is bad for the physical, mental, and emotional health of the body and is directly related to the infant mortality rate. She began this exploration in the context of studying the unusually high labor and delivery complications experienced by Black women, regardless of education, socioeconomic status, or quality of health care, and concluded that the natural stress of birthing is compounded by the added toxic stress of systemic discrimination and racism. Geronimus theorized that this phenomenon of weathering demonstrated the corrosive effects of racism on Black bodies already damaged by living in America. Her study and others published in *The New England Journal of Medicine* (Kenneth Schoendorf et al., cited in Villarosa 73) and the *Journal of Health and Social Behavior* (David Williams, cited in Villarosa 76) underscore the relationship between racism, discrimination, and adverse health consequences on Black people. This research generated the hypothesis that if you're the subject of that toxicity, historically, every time something racially oppressive happens, such as being the target of discrimination, the systems of your body rev up, whether it's your heart rate, your blood pressure, the stress hormones, or even if it's everyday stress—someone questions your competence despite your credentials, follows you around in a store, or people recoil when you enter an elevator—your body reacts, storing the repeated stress over time and creating a kind of accelerated aging.

If we add the additional challenges found in roles where Black women are the first and/or the only Black person, the weathering impact operates in a similar fashion. That is, over time the normal stressors of leadership intersect with the stressors of being Black and a woman to the detriment of their physical bodies as well as their mental and emotional well-being. What does weathering look like for these leaders? We propose that when Black women take on executive level roles in higher education, weathering is compounded by an environment that exploits diversity and inclusion while simultaneously encouraging and condoning the very microaggressions that cause weathering. Their experiences are present-day examples of the phenomena documented in studies done by Geronimus, by her mentor Sherman James (Villarosa 83), and by other researchers recorded in Linda Villarosa's powerful book *Under the Skin: The Hidden Toll of Racism on American Lives and on the Health of Our Nation*. Building on her thesis about how structural inequalities based on race affect the health of Black lives regardless of social class or education, we suggest that Black women who possess the necessary cultural capital to succeed in high-risk administrative roles encounter instead assaults on their credentials, intellectual capacity, and ability to enact the role effectively, resulting in a deleterious impact on their physical state across contexts.

As part of this weathering process for Black women as leaders, other even more astringent assaults occur. To illustrate, the institution hires these administrators with the explicit understanding that it wants to use them to bring about a change in a department, school, or college that may be, at worst, experiencing stagnation or the potential for downsizing or, at best, may be moving toward raising its national ranking or increasing the visibility of a college or other unit within the institution. Into this morass walk the highly sought-after and courted leaders of color, or, in our cases, the first Black women in those positions in the history of our respective institutions. Although the universities had no difficulty celebrating our uniqueness and their own acumen and foresight in bringing such diversity to an existing traditional role, at the same time we often faced extraordinary resistance that impeded changes we proposed. As an example, if you design a revenue-generating plan based on the requirements of your direct reportee, you might suddenly be told you must secure the review and approval of several other cooperating units and, even if you have already taken that step, you might then be informed that you will not have authority to control the generated funds. By embracing this approach, the institution can "have it both ways," claiming to address inclusion and make changes, while simultaneously using authority and title, absent a justifiable reason or purpose, to block your agency and empowerment. Maintenance of that status quo, despite the heralded entrance of the Black woman leader, allows the institution to stymy any transformations that she seeks to undertake.

Adopting this strategy may be likened to the courtship rituals endemic to many cultural traditions in which assiduous and even ardent pursuit of the desired partner appears to signal a genuine hope for a lasting relationship, that is, marriage. Thus, in their seemingly unqualified embrace of our presence and openness to our proposed modifications, the institutions can use us as "diversity window dressing" without ever committing to the innovations that would signal our inclusion and the institution's genuine desire to partner with us in implementing needed adjustments to outdated policies and practices.

On the other hand, existing simultaneously with this uneasy "courtship of change" resides a subliminal and biased assumption that you are not quite up to the task of leading even the most mundane of change initiatives. While seeming to laud your extraordinary suitability for the role, the stereotypes, systemic racism, and sexism enacted at both the individual and institutional levels threaten any genuine attempts you make to build a collaborative and evolving context for change purposely intended to build sustainable outcomes that will outlive your tenure. Instead, the first Black woman leader may find herself constantly confronting unseen barriers she did not know existed in conflict with the evolutionary change the institution claimed it wished her to initiate and promote. She runs up against what philosopher Charles Mills refers to as unwritten and unspoken but understood and embraced laws of the Racial Contract between whites and based on the "unnamed political system" of white supremacy (1–7).

To be sure, any steps toward transformational change within an institution will, of necessity, involve resistance—not rooted in systemic inequities, but rather due to the push and pull of the loss of what is known versus the potential gain of the unknown. Prepared leaders know this regardless of the multiple identities they bring to the role. For the Black woman, however, the push and pull involves a much more insidious and potentially damaging reality—that is, the intersectionality of race, gender, sexual orientation, class, age, physical ability, and perhaps even religion. That is a crucial difference between what you see and what you don't and is a strong contributor to the weathering in leadership that Black women experience. Indeed, we argue, it would not be an exaggeration to suggest that this weathering is yet another form of post-traumatic syndrome, with all of the attendant traumas and complications. Any trauma leaves a lasting mark on the human psyche; some of the effects are obvious and readily identified, while others are unseen but no less damaging. The effects emerge in unexpected and unpredictable ways for the traumatized individual. Perhaps the most problematic is intergenerational institutional trauma—the kind that, in Villarosa's term, lurks under the skin.

If we are to lessen the likelihood that would-be Black women leaders die in the chrysalis rather than emerge in the full beauty of their potential and individuality, we must admit and confront the experiences that undermine their competence, self-esteem, and ability to thrive. For that reason, the notion that one must wait for a critical mass or pipeline of potential leaders to appear fails to acknowledge the flaws in the surroundings that thwart even the most gifted of these leaders. This requires us to engage with potential leaders at various levels in academia to plan for diversity in succession by building intergenerational capacity. It is precisely for that reason that we have chosen to include in this volume the perspectives and experiences of Black women from emerging to seasoned leaders navigating the contested terrain of leadership in the academy.

FROM THE GLASS CEILING TO THE GLASS CLIFF

For decades women have talked about shattering the glass ceiling in order to take their rightful places in leadership roles in the workplace. The term, coined in 1978 by Marilyn Loden at a panel discussion on women's fettered career aspirations, refers primarily to the impenetrable barriers in corporate enterprises that leave them trailing behind white males who dominate executive levels of organizations. Over the years, that imbalance has changed dramatically for white women in a broad variety of professions, yet despite the creation of a federal Glass Ceiling Commission (1991–1996), obstacles to advancement still remain.

The phenomenon of the glass ceiling has been shadowed and further complicated by the concept of the glass escalator, a metaphor used by Christine Williams in her study of the advantages for men in what traditionally have been considered professions geared toward women, for example, nurses, elementary school teachers, librarians, and social workers. Based on interviews of men and women in those professions, she concludes that despite the fact that men are underrepresented in these occupations and can experience tokenism and discrimination, in particular from people outside the profession, they often enjoy a decided advantage in that the responses from the men and women interviewed suggest that "men are given fair—if not preferential—treatment in hiring and promotion decisions, are accepted by supervisors and colleagues, and are well integrated into the work place subculture"; and even where the men feel pushed out of those professions, the prejudice they experience can lead them "into more 'legitimate' (and higher paying) occupations" (264). Although Black women are capable of riding the escalator for advancement, the problem is that they are unprepared for the built-in stops that delay or even detour their ability to reach the top at the same rate as less marginalized groups.

The presumed egalitarian escalator is yet another metaphor for failures within systemic inequities at every level of leadership. Some of them you can clearly identify while others are implied and thereby elusive, but are not immediately perceived because they are so much a part of the normative fabric of the system, such as when you are left out of conversations about your own unit as well as related units, or have information withheld about significant decisions being made that will affect your unit. For that reason, if we are to have a sustainable, thriving leadership that is diverse and inclusive, it is essential to consider the pitfalls not only for those who have attained leadership roles but also for emerging leaders to thrive within a system grounded in racial and social justice.

Black women who do succeed in riding the escalator to the top and breaking the glass ceiling at various executive levels are very often ultimately faced with a third obstacle that impedes their success, and that is the glass cliff. Michelle K. Ryan and S. Alexander Haslam address this experience in a study hypothesizing that women who climb the corporate ladder and who attain leadership roles face the invisible barrier of the glass cliff, whereby in contrast to the preponderance of their male counterparts, they are very closely and critically scrutinized, often experience unfairly harsh evaluations, and find that their "positions are risky and precarious" (81). Ryan and Haslam conjecture that in addition to the problems that women face related to assumptions about their gender, they often are appointed to problematic and unstable leadership positions that are likely to be less promising than those of their male counterparts. They conclude the study with three very significant recommendations concerning female leaders—namely, that (1) it is essential to shed light on how female leaders "may be differentially exposed to criticism and in greater danger of being apportioned blame for negative outcomes that were set in train well before they assumed their new roles"; (2) we must explore "the nature of the corporate motivations underlying the appointment of women to precarious positions"; and (3) "it is also necessary to establish whether the glass cliff phenomenon extends outside the boardroom and into other leadership arenas" (87).

These recommendations fall in line with what we as leaders and the contributors to the volume have experienced as Black women in higher education and account, in great part, for the inequities throughout the hierarchy in academic leadership, which is no less perilous or riveted than that of the corporate board room, built on systemic inequities driven by power, privilege, implicit bias, and more recently, hastily and poorly conceived attempts to address demands for diversity and inclusion in the workplace. Instead, institutions often focus on increasing the numbers of people of color rather than setting goals for sustaining their presence and supporting their success; on performative displays of celebrating diversity rather than on revising policies that reflect changed mindsets and demonstrated commitments to recognizing the accomplishments of their hires who are working to break down barriers; and on resisting changes that address the complicity of the status quo in its failure to remove these barriers rather than accepting and embracing structural changes needed to address systemic inequities in, for instance, hiring processes and how those hired are trained, mentored, and evaluated.

In the absence of changes to these misperceptions, Black women often are left immersed in a conundrum in which they are striving to maintain secure footing in a position that is very "slippery and perilous to navigate" as they attempt to lead within "a space of whiteness . . . without the guidance afforded others" (Hodges and Welch, "Dilemmas of Deaning" 67) because their capabilities and accomplishments are questioned or ignored, or they are defined by controlling images characterizing them as angry and overbearing when they question the system. Such a position is even more challenging for those who are the first Black administrators in the position, who, while on display as firsts representing a victory for their race, are led to feel, in interactions with their counterparts, as though their race and gender position them as being mislaid or temporarily lost.

For Black women leaders, the glass cliff presents obstacles occasioned by multiple intersecting exclusionary challenges often obscured by what

Beverly Tatum refers to as the racial smog that all Americans traverse and to which many become inured and oblivious. She explains, "Cultural racism—the cultural images and messages that affirm the assumed inferiority of people of color—is like smog in the air. Sometimes it is so thick, it is visible, other times it is less apparent, but always, day in and day out, we are breathing it in" (6). Smog of any kind makes landscapes indistinct and, therefore, difficult to identify and maneuver. In the United States, the smog of systemic racism is so deeply an interwoven reality in the multiple daily contexts in which we operate that it too does not rise to the conscious level needed to initiate dialogue that would address it. Thus, too often, it falls to Black people to become the canaries in the racist, American coalmines that exist at multiple levels. Racial smog makes many people blind to institutionalized and systemic advantages for the white majority that create severe disparities for the minoritized and allow some among the majority to become "diversity actors" who display their commitment in a performative manner, by which they rely on celebrations of diversity and displays of unity that are short-lived and offer no changes in the existing structure nor impose concerted measures of accountability. Not only do the minoritized individuals lose but no one really wins, and the racial smog persists.

Additionally, the persistence of the racial smog allows for the glass cliff to perpetuate the inequities across the terrain of leadership inhabited by Black women administrators. For white women, the glass cliff is certainly also slippery, and likewise contested for them as for Black women. For Black women, however, there are additional challenges that must be acknowledged. The glass cliff on which Black women find themselves is one where being Black constitutes an onerous enigma, that is, when their presence is noted and experienced as part of the leadership team, they find themselves viewed as what Deborah Gray White sees as a "disquieting disruption of convention" (6). Addressing this predicament in reflections on her position as a Black woman scholar from a PWI presenting at a large, prestigious conference, White characterizes this feeling as being "matter out of place," that is, she notes that race and gender make her an anomaly and that "I would have to prove that I was in fact in the right place" (5).

Black women leaders on the glass cliff essentially come to be seen as a disruption to convention rather than a new, potentially transformative face of leadership. Even though they initially might be welcomed as the "trophy" diversity addition recommended for the stellar accomplishments and skills they bring to the position, they eventually are seen as, and sense themselves to be matter out of place when their accomplishments and proposals are not positively acknowledged and are perhaps even viewed askance. In this case, they grapple with the "pet to threat" phenomenon coined by Kecia Thomas, a Black dean who introduced the idea in a presentation where she talked about barriers to advancement of women of color in higher education. Ciarra Jones describes Thomas's characterization in this way:

> [there is] an evolution of professional discrimination for women of color. In the early "pet" stage, women are tokenized, coddled, and underestimated—often trotted out as "diversity and inclusion" show ponies, while at the same time dismissed and distrusted with important work that would let them grow. As people grow and become proficient—despite the disinvestment—then comes the threat stage . . . [when they] become a threat to the status quo, and can experience career roadblocks, lack of advancement, and being denied recognition for their achievements. (Jones)

The Black woman takes on the administrative role with a double standard already in place that is both seen and unseen. Thomas presents the syndrome as one that evolves from early to late career, and certainly, the further you advance the more difficult it becomes. Yet we submit that it can happen cyclically, that is, at various stages and intensities in one's career depending on the contexts in which you operate at any given time. For us, it is the reality that no matter what achievements one does score, you nevertheless feel as though you are starting anew and having to repeatedly prove that you are the right person in the right place. To traverse this terrain, then, requires Black women to engage in a kind of mental gymnastics, which Du Bois labeled double consciousness, or "twoness," with the "sense of always looking at oneself through the eyes of others," (3) that is, navigating between the two worlds of oppressed and oppressor, an exercise that intensifies the impact of weathering.

All too often, Black women who prevail in enacting their roles while overcoming their struggles as administrators are saddled with the stereotypical assumption that it is a measure of their resilience, a form of exceptionalism that has propelled them through the glass ceiling. Indeed, resilience is a factor, but focusing on it as a chief factor of success threatens to erase the long-term effects of violations of self and identity they encounter in the workplace and diminishes their ability to withstand obstacles and turn their pain into action. Resilience is no substitute for equality. Those who succeed do so not because they are able to passively endure assaults on their character; rather, it is because, despite the trauma, they affirm an active stance within survival mode. They draw on their pain to function and to create a new reality. In some ways, Black women are expected to accept erasure. Yet they simply want to live and contribute in meaningful ways—to be seen, heard, and treated as fully functioning human beings, without the baggage of shallow prejudices. As with the historical context of their enslaved ancestors, their positions are dictated by uncertainty as they deal with "a past that is not past [but] reappears, always to rupture the present" (Sharpe 9). They do not want to be regarded as exceptional, resilient Black women but instead want to be accepted as the norm and not as "matter out of place." Nor will they settle for erasure in the service of occupying a secure position on the cliff.

In the absence of that egalitarian framework, Black women maneuvering across the glass cliff keep that seemingly elusive goal in focus by adopting a position best described by Sarah Amira de la Garza as a praxis of courage called mindful heresy, which "creates a resistant framework, like a protective shawl, for continued dignified expression of my intelligence and my contributions" (202). Based on her experiences in the academy as a Hispanic doctoral student who suffered a disability as a result of an accident that posed obstacles throughout her career, de la Garza explains how she calls on inspiring words of her living elders and memories of her ancestors from whom she draws courage and strength. She explains,

> A heretic by tradition, is an outcast, who leaves, hides, and/or camouflages to avoid the negative repercussions of her heresy. What makes the mindful heretic stand apart is the refusal to depart, the continued public affiliation while demonstrating a failure to comply with the orthodoxy, and the refusal to internalize or accept orthodox framings of one's status in (here) the academy. (202)

Several times she uses the word orthodoxy, which, for us, represents the challenges of the status quo or slippery glass cliff on which many Black women tread.

For Black women leaders, using our own form of mindful heresy, grounded in traditions stemming from our African legacy and experiences that are reminders of the history of our enslaved ancestors in the United States and of our understanding of double consciousness, is just the beginning for reimagining leadership and more firmly securing and prevailing in positions within the academic administrative hierarchy. It is a means of developing an oppositional stance as a challenge to the traditional canons of leadership preparation and development. This bearing also illustrates a way to help redirect the conversations on leadership in which we engage to close the divide or gap and construct an equal playing field on which we interact with our white colleagues and other colleagues of color.

RECONCEPTUALIZING THE
NARRATIVE ON LEADERSHIP

The position of Black women in higher education leadership calls for radical changes whereby a new, broadened norm must be understood that challenges, removes, and revises restrictive policies and practices of hiring, evaluation, support for, and engagement with a diverse set of individuals and demands radical changes on two major levels. First, central to the necessary changes are revised policies and practices that address systemic racism and become a part of the institutional structure. But that change cannot be achieved by providing lip service to diversity and inclusion. Institutional leaders must engage with faculty and staff to reimagine the narrative on leadership in ways that lead them to create a new vision of the "norm," one that, in reality, deconstructs the idea of "normal" through the genuine broad inclusivity it supports. Rewriting the narrative on leadership means, as a first step, accepting the wisdom of Black women leaders and applying concerted efforts to move away from doing things the way they always have been done and abandoning in some measure the comfort of business as usual. That leads to the second step, which is to enact meaningful change that fully promotes a culture of inclusion in ways clearly demonstrated in the operation of the institution's mission and vision. As Black women who were pioneers from their race in our positions, we often thought about what happens when the institution does not broaden diversity and simply replicates the existing model. We realized that no matter how salient or compelling our vision for change, the fact that we were the messengers would almost certainly, at worst, doom it to failure and, at best, and perhaps more galling, have that vision appropriated and placed in the hands of a messenger deemed to be a "better fit."

Chief on our minds was the issue of what is lost in terms of potential if that vision is not revisited, and we concluded that "given the current social and political climate and the obstacles that it presents to individuals based on gender, race and ethnicity, sexual orientation, and disability, it is imperative that we take a discerning look at how leaders are chosen and asked to operate" (Hodges and Welch, "The Face of Leadership" 2). This notion compels us to emphasize the reality that the reimagination, like the impulse to eradicate racism, is never finally complete; it is an ongoing task, a continuing work in progress, if you will, for which we must constantly be mindful of the past in adjusting to the ever-changing future. This is particularly important to keep in mind for Black women in PWIs as well as those for who hire them.

For us and the contributors to this volume, it means acknowledging the historical links and voices of leadership that since the nineteenth century have addressed the very issues surrounding the contemporary disputes about diversity and inclusion, namely, ongoing challenges of racism in a broad array of contexts, threats to affirmative action, denial of the problems related to intersectionality, and spurious attacks on critical race theory as a form of reverse racism. Higher education has long imagined itself exemplary and above the fray of those resistant to these ideas, but it has not been able to provide a reasonable defense of the failures to resolve those very problems within its own structure. Furthermore, politicians and other national leaders jostling for power and presence have forced these issues to the forefront in higher education where, in particular at many PWIs, institutional leaders eager to appease their supporters have struggled to divest themselves of their past exclusionary reputations and make sustainable changes in concert with milestones achieved in the name of civil rights. Regrettably, some of those milestones have been erased or are now under threat, making it harder for Black women leaders to bring and sustain change.

Thirty years ago, Derrick Bell claimed that "racism in America is not a curable aberration . . . rather, it is a key component in this country's stability" (x). His words not only recall Du Bois's prescient warning at the turn of the twentieth century about the color line as a dominant national and international problem of the century but also remind us that the activism of Black women "iron butterflies" along the way offers lessons for the current and ongoing uneasy racial dynamics in the United States in general and higher education in particular.

Leaders focused on minding the gap reject false and oversimplified binaries (for example, racist vs not racist) in which civility often becomes the overriding determinant to define one's commitment to diversity and inclusion and for bridging the gap precipitated by difference. Civility or mere tolerance is not a tool from which we can construct a solution for what divides us, especially when entrenched systems of injustice pervade too many higher education institutions. In these contexts, the emphasis placed on encouraging civil dialogue is often proposed as the only means through which to confront the quagmire of racism, but it offers, instead, a weak substitute for a more radical, transformative approach. Dr. Martin Luther King, Jr.'s renowned and highly effective role as a civil rights activist evolved from a position of nonviolent protest and politics of civility to a leadership stance that incorporated the idea of the radical revolutionaries engaged in civic radicalism, which has been highlighted as "the crown jewel of [King's] legacy" (Zamalin 2). In his 1963 "Letter From Birmingham Jail," King wrote about the failure of civility in attaining civil rights legislation, because, "King thought that his 'greatest stumbling block' was not the Ku Klux Klan member but the white moderate basking in civility, the rules of which dictated compromise and mutual respect" (Zamalin 72).

In higher education as well, efforts to promote civility to address racial conflict in the academy often masquerade as the only means to repair racial division within the social climate. Zamalin suggests that a persistent and hidden racism exists in the obsession with civility that masks any discourse about racial justice (7). This convenient and all too comfortable civil stance, or "hegemony of niceness" (De la Garza 202) may provide a polite convention that supports the persistence of racial smog around discussions of leadership, particularly when they center on how Black women enact their roles. The mask of civility donned by those who seek to eradicate racism and those who seek to defend it detracts from the kind of engagement required to critically examine higher education leadership. In short, civility can be assumed as an effective way to insulate one from any criticism that a promotion of injustice is occurring or that the choices hurt others (Zamalin 7).

We are not the first to argue that arousing discomfort with the way things have always been handled is a key starting point for dialogue around the ways things *could be* in higher education administration. Such a dialogue is critical if the gap for Black women leaders is ever to be authentically confronted and addressed. Radical revolutionaries engage in actions that push forcefully against established binaries and maintenance of an unquestioned status quo. They envision a social canvas on which equality and justice intertwine. Such an intertwining addresses racial disparities in academic leadership in a holistic, institutional fashion, whereby the promotion of social and racial justice becomes everyone's responsibility and is not just under the purview of offices focusing on diversity and inclusion.

Thus, to mind the gap in a higher education setting means undertaking a deliberative investigation and interrogation of an institution's history, how it enacts its mission, and how it formulates its vision for the future. For example, some institutions try to do this by counting numbers annually in terms of diversity but that does not address the issue and requires a longer-term view about several aspects of campus life. A more productive approach applies intense scrutiny to its student, faculty, and staff recruitment and to how to provide resources and design strategic planning that will over time build and sustain the numbers. In short, building for sustainable diverse engagement and collaboration across the institution linked to an ongoing evolution of its vision and mission must eschew quick fixes and bait-and-switch attention gimmicks in favor of authentic and sometimes disquieting conversations across multiple disciplines and human experiences required for earnest engagement in structural institutional change.

It is evolution and engagement that incorporate an authentic and critical examination and recognition of historical precedent in one's institution, and that embrace approaches that consistently and consciously challenge long-standing, traditionally accepted ways of operating that have too long been accepted as unassailable and immutable. This means launching a radical revolution of sorts, at both macro and micro levels, that intentionally invites questions and dialogues across difference and generates actions arising from those conversations. Viewed from Audre Lorde's perspective, when she addressed issues related to Black and white women in conflict, this tactic allows us to use our differences as a tool that becomes a fund of interdependence, by which we can gain "the power to seek new ways of being [and] the courage and sustenance to act where there are no charters" ("Master's Tools" 111). Lorde advocates for embracing difference as a tool representing strength that flourishes through mutual dependence and heightens the possibility to transform the communities in which we live and the contexts in which we work. She points out,

> Those of us who have been forged on the crucibles of difference . . . know that *survival is not an academic skill*. It is learning how to stand alone, unpopular and sometimes reviled, and how to make common cause with those others identified as outside the structures to define and seek a world in which we all flourish. For the master's tools will never dismantle the master's house. They may allow us temporarily to beat him at his own game, but they will never enable us to bring about genuine change. And this fact is only threatening to those women who still define the master's house as the only source of support. ("Master's Tools" 112)

Key to Lorde's theme of mutual dependence that is founded on embracing difference and building a community of trust is the need to redefine difference, which people tend to view through lenses exposing "old blueprints of expectations and response [and] old structures of oppression" ("Women Redefining Difference" 123) that stifle self-definition and make it difficult to change. She concludes that "[w]e sharpen self-definition by exposing self in work and struggle together with those whom we define as different from ourselves, although sharing the same goals. For Black and white, old and young, lesbian and heterosexual women alike, this can mean new paths to our survival" (123). Academic administrators seeking to create new paths for building communities of trust and mutual dependence across differences must relinquish the centrality of the ego that builds a twisted narrative around itself to the detriment of the institution and fails to see all of the institutional possibilities for positive change. The ego robs the leader of the ability to be both/and, that is, to be in two places at the same time, functioning from the perspective of double-consciousness, a strength that Black women bring to the institution through their ability to see and be seen without jeopardizing the mission or vision of any higher education context.

SEEKING TRANSFORMATION THROUGH A WEB OF MUTUALITY

We believe that Lorde's idea of redefining and embracing difference applies to a reimagining of the institution based on a web of mutuality. A strategy proposed by Heather McGhee in her insightful work, *The Sum of Us: What Racism Costs Everyone and How We Can Prosper Together,* affirms how difference can be a tool for dismantling racism. She echoes and builds upon Lorde's idea of redefining and embracing difference in her insistence that "a functioning society rests on a web of mutuality, a willingness among all involved to share enough with one another to accomplish what no one person can do alone" (34). For this strategy to succeed in higher education, however, a rethinking of how leadership is defined and practiced must occur, including an interrogation of its deep-rooted hierarchies and outdated definition and application of meritocracy and policies, its understanding of diversity and inclusion, and an intentional, concerted commitment to transform the vision of leadership. Such a goal recognizes that discussions surrounding higher education leadership cannot be formulated like a cookbook recipe, replete with fixed formulaic ingredients and steps. Instead, leaders can and must be expected to mind the gap by placing transparency, inclusion, and racial and social justice in the forefront of their thinking about and enactment of the leadership role. For this strategy to succeed, a rethinking of how higher education in general and/or leadership in particular is practiced must occur.

Throughout this chapter, we have given examples of how Black women leaders in the academy operate within what Melissa Harris-Perry refers to as spaces with a "crooked chair in a crooked room" (28), which they attempt to make straight by using both conventional and unconventional strategies. The unconventional strategies include lessons from their African heritage as well as those specific and unique lessons learned from being Black in America. However, no matter how well schooled one may be, there is no panacea for the hidden racism that confronts even the most intelligent, competent, and well-prepared Black women leaders in higher education. Moreover, the insistence on civil discourse allows misinformation and obfuscation to remain largely unchallenged. For us, minding the gap in higher education leadership calls for activism captured in King's focus on a radical revolution of values and civic radicalism. It proposes erecting an egalitarian framework of higher education leadership in which all can thrive and supports the unapologetic, antiracist transformation of leadership by Black women that we and the contributors to this volume envision.

In the nineteenth and twentieth centuries, two devoted and highly esteemed champions of racial justice, W. E. B. Du Bois and Derek Bell, warned us about the ubiquitous and inexorable impact of racism, and we have seen it played out in the misuses and abuses of the concepts of

race and skin color. Many writers have reminded us that race is a social construct based on rules and not rooted in biological evidence and
that whiteness as well is a powerful cultural invention. In the preface to
his work *The Possessive Investment in Whiteness*, Lipsitz points out that
whiteness, a long-held social fact, is "cultural fiction" and "delusion" and
refers to it again in a chapter to which he gives the title "A Pigment of the
Imagination" (vii). Thus, in seeking to repair a divide that has engendered
conflict and dissonance and to redress the resulting grievances wrought
globally and nationally, it is critical to center our gaze in the twenty-first
century on the role of higher education in general and academic leadership in particular as sources for transformational change. Safiya Noble,
who had a career in marketing and advertising before becoming a university professor, reminds us that advances in human knowledge not only
can help us but also can unwittingly complicate our struggles for social
justice in her insightful study *Algorithms of Oppression: How Search Engines Reinforce Racism*, focusing on "the power of algorithms in the age
of neoliberalism and the ways those digital decisions reinforce oppressive social relationships, and enact new modes of racial profiling, which
I have termed technological redlining" (1). The quick growth and prom-
inence of artificial intelligence (AI) has heralded brilliant contributions
in many areas, for instance, solutions for medical ailments or agricul-
tural failures, but Noble warns against too much reliance on automated
decisions. She notes that

> [p]art of the challenge of understanding algorithmic oppression is to
> understand that mathematical formulations to drive automated deci-
> sions are made by human beings. While we often think of terms such
> as "big data" and "algorithms" as being benign, neutral, or objective, they
> are anything but. The people who make these decisions hold all types of
> values, many of which openly promote racism, sexism, and false notions
> of meritocracy, which is well documented in studies of Silicon Valley. (1)

An example of her concern is explicitly demonstrated in an analysis of how three thousand AI images essentially reduced the world to stereotypes. Turk calls our attention to the need for "minding the gaps" in human relations that govern racial and social justice in society at large and particularly in higher education leadership. We include this to say that "othering" in any context is dangerous, as it closes possibilities and potential for evolutionary change that can benefit everyone.

We and our contributors seek to elucidate the particular experiences of Black women administrators at a variety of levels in academic leadership as a means of animating what we hope opens new spaces for dialogue on best practices in higher education leadership and carves out places where what is brought to the table in terms of difference is valued and included rather than dismissed or co-opted. In advancing this vision, we do not suggest a utopian view of the myriad requirements and challenges faced by any administrator in higher education. Rather, we call for spaces and places where Black women leaders can BE BLACK without having to PROVE BLACK, where they can experience leadership with no groundless assaults on their integrity, where they are valued for their integrity above their academic pedigree, and where integrity is an absolute expectation for engagement, inclusion, and assessment for themselves and those with whom they interact. The more stories we have of those who enter leadership from positions typically viewed as non-traditional by virtue of race, class, physical ability, or sexual orientation, the better we can begin to understand and make adjustments to the elusive nature of leadership for Black American women and other minoritized populations across academic contexts.

WORKS CITED

American Museum of Natural History. "Butterfly Metamorphosis." https://www.amnh.org/exhibitions/butterflies/metamorphosis.

Bell, Derrick. *Faces at the Bottom of the Well: The Permanence of Racism*. Basic Books, 1992.

De la Garza, Sarah Amira. "Mindful Heresy as Praxis for Change: Responding to Microaggressions as Building Blocks of Hegemony." *Presumed Incompetent II. Race, Class, Power, and Resistance of Women in Academia*, edited by Yolanda Flores Niemann et al., Utah State UP, 2020, pp. 193–203.

Du Bois, W. E. B. *The Souls of Black Folk: Essays and Sketches*. Dodd, Mead, 1979.

Geronimus, Arline. "The Weathering Hypothesis and the Health of African-American Women and Infants: Evidence and Speculations." *Ethnicity & Disease*, vol. 2, no. 3, summer 1992, pp. 207–21.

Harris-Perry, Melissa. *Sister Citizen: Shame, Stereotypes, and Black Women in America*. Yale UP, 2011.

Hodges, Carolyn R., and Olga M. Welch. "Making Noise and Good, Necessary Trouble: Dilemmas of Deaning While Black." *Dismantling Institutional Whiteness: Emerging Forms of Leadership in Higher Education*, edited by M. Cristina Alcalde and Mangala Subramaniam, Purdue UP, 2023, pp. 55–75.

———. "The Face of Leadership." *Education Week*, 30 May 2018, https://ew.edweek.org/nxtbooks/epe/ew_05302018/index.php?startid=23#/p/22.

Jones, Ciarra. "Corporate Workplaces Are Traumatizing Black Women." *Elite Daily*, 11 Oct. 2022, https://www.elitedaily.com/news/pet-to-threat-early-career-impact.

Lipsitz, George. "A Pigment of the Imagination." *The Possessive Investment in Whiteness: How White People Profit from Identity Politics*. Twentieth Anniversary ed., Temple UP, 2018, pp. 147–60.

Loden, Marilyn. "100 Women: 'Why I Invented the Glass Ceiling Phrase.'" *BBC News*, 12 Dec. 2017, https://www.bbc.com/news/world-42026266.

Lorde, Audre. "The Master's Tools will Never Dismantle the Master's House." *Sister Outsider: Essays and Speeches by Audre Lorde*. Crossing Press, 1984, pp. 110–13.

———. "Age, Race, Class, and Sex: Women Redefining Difference." *Sister*

Outsider: Essays and Speeches by Audre Lorde. Crossing Press, 1984, pp. 114–23.

McGhee, Heather. *The Sum of Us: What Racism Costs Everyone and How We Can Prosper Together.* One World, 2021.

Mills, Charles W. *The Racial Contract.* Twenty-fifth anniversary edition. Cornell UP, 2022.

Noble, Safiya. *Algorithms of Oppression: How Search Engines Reinforce Racism.* NYUP, 2018.

Ryan, Michelle K., and S. Alexander Haslam. "The Glass Cliff: Evidence that Women are Over-Represented in Precarious Leadership Positions." *British Journal of Management,* vol. 16, 2005, pp. 81–90. Wiley Online Library, https://doi.org/10.1111/j.1467-8551.2005.00433.x.

Sharpe, Christina. *In the Wake: On Blackness and Being.* Duke UP, 2016.

Tatum, Beverly. *"Why Are All the Black Kids Sitting Together in the Cafeteria?" and Other Conversations about Race.* Basic Books, 1997.

Turk, Victoria. "How AI Reduces the World to Stereotypes." *Rest of World,* 10 Oct. 2023, https://restofworld.org/2023/ai-image-stereotypes.

Villarosa, Linda. *Under the Skin: The Hidden Toll of Racism on American Lives and on the Health of Our Nation.* Doubleday, 2022.

White, Deborah Gray. "'Matter Out of Place': Ar'n't I a Woman? Black Female Scholars and the Academy." Women, Slavery, and Historical Research, special issue of *The Journal of African American History,* edited by Brenda E. Stevenson, vol. 92, no. 1, winter 2007, pp. 5–12.

Williams, Christine L. "The Glass Escalator: Hidden Advantages for Men in the 'Female Professions.'" *Social Problems,* vol. 39, no. 3, Aug. 1992, pp. 253–67. JSTOR, www.jstor.org/stable/3096961.

Zamalin, Alex. *Against Civility: The Hidden Racism in Our Obsession with Civility.* Beacon Press, 2021.

2

THE DEI CONUNDRUM FOR BLACK WOMEN LEADERS

Stephanie J. Rowley

t is hard to describe the intensity of the emotions that I experienced myself and witnessed in others in the days immediately following George Floyd's murder. I was devastated by the lack of regard for human life, for Black life. Liberal white colleagues were especially affected by the murder, their feelings likely amplified because they were quarantined at home with little to do other than watch news coverage of the horrific incident and because they were experiencing simultaneously the rawness of the human experience exposed through a deadly global pandemic. As provost and dean of the oldest graduate school of education in the country, Teachers College, Columbia University, I not only was concerned about my own well-being but also was thinking of how to support members of our community who were deeply affected and angry, feeling disconnected because of the COVID shutdowns. I was not surprised by student and faculty demands that the College denounce the act and reflect on our commitments to racial justice. I was, however, surprised by the handful of white women who reached out to ask, "how I was doing" and to offer their help. One even apologized for not being more helpful to me earlier.

The gestures were problematic for me for a few reasons. These were not women with whom I had worked closely or was friendly. Thus, their gestures felt superficial, the "performative allyship" (10) described by Amponsah and Stephen. It did not seem that these liberal colleagues were wrestling with the reality of white supremacy so much as struggling with their feelings of individual guilt (Spanierman). Ironically, assuaging their guilt by offering help to me served to center whiteness and their comfort (Thompson), even while they likely felt virtuous and anti-racist. The offers also demonstrated a paternalism that we face as Black women leaders. I am confident that these women would not have offered solace to my white or Black male counterparts under similar circumstances. In essence, I became the Black woman dean, and rather than feeling supported or more visible in the face of these offers of help, I felt othered and pitied. This experience captures for me one dilemma of being a Black woman in a leadership role. I was hired, in part, for my commitment to diversity, equity, and inclusion (DEI), but some colleagues' diversity values were perverted into pity and white guilt.

This chapter will take on several issues related to what I call the DEI dilemma for Black women leaders; that is, the manner in which increasing numbers of Black women leaders reflect institutional commitments to diversity, even as women leaders are often handed insurmountable tasks and as their ability to lead effectively is undermined by resistance to diversity, equity, and inclusion efforts.

Lest I imply that opportunities for Black women to lead in higher education are lacking, I will begin by discussing how this watershed moment—shaped by the national racial reckoning and the COVID-19 pandemic—also has the potential to seed real change in higher education. These new leaders form a cohort of Black women and will visibly and culturally change the face of the academy. In addition, I will reflect on the concept of the "glass cliff," the circumstance whereby Black women are asked to lead institutions after the emergence of a crisis, sometimes under precarious conditions and with few resources. Next, I will address the tension between the critical DEI skills that Black women have honed by necessity and the expectation that they serve in a "mammy" role, nurturing those who are marginalized and delivering healing where trust has been broken. In conclusion, this chapter will offer insights into these tensions, but also provide some suggestions for institutions and new leaders.

THE RACIAL RECKONING AND
BLACK WOMEN'S MOMENT

The murders of George Floyd, Breanna Taylor, Ahmaud Arbery, and others led to a national reckoning across the country and in institutions of higher education. There was no way to ignore the realities of race as lived in the United States. Individuals of all backgrounds responded to the call to arms to be better, to educate themselves, to engage in anti-racist behavior, and to demand equity and inclusion in higher education. In the summer after Floyd's murder, white support for the Black Lives Matter movement increased from about forty percent to about sixty percent (Spanierman). In addition to a proliferation of race-related book clubs and white ally groups, higher education responded with a spate of "diversity" hiring, a trend mirrored in corporate America (Elias; Ellis 2). Even as the job market stalled more generally because of the COVID-19 pandemic, applicants studying issues of race, ethnicity, and culture were in high demand. There was also a notable trend for universities to hire Black leaders, including deans, provosts, and presidents. In the months between June 2020 and November 2021, over twenty-five percent of all US college presidents hired were Black women, versus about fifteen percent in the three years leading up to 2020 (Lederman).

There has been a similar trend in hiring deans. For example, in 2022, there were four Black women from my previous institution, a school of education, named major leaders (one president, three deans, including myself) at other institutions in a single year. The numbers at Teachers College are more rule than exception. At this time, in 2023, seven of sixty (twelve percent) deans of education schools in the Association of American Universities are Black women. In 2022, more than thirteen percent of law school deans (28/207 queried) were Black women (Norwood). This number was more than double the number of Black men and half of all women law school deans. The numbers of Black women law deans also eclipsed numbers of Latina (n = 5) and Asian American (n = 3) women law deans. Harold and Livingston similarly found that half of all law schools in Illinois were led by Black women in 2022. As of 2018, Harvard had four Black women deans and one of those, Claudine Gay, went on to become the first Black woman president of Harvard.

The critical mass of Black women leaders can have far-reaching implications. One can imagine shifts in our collective ideas about what a dean looks like—the gut-level sense that shapes beliefs about the characteristics of strong leadership and the insights of search committees. One of the most prominent examples of the power of representation is in US Vice President Kamala Harris. Harris's election was widely viewed as confirmation that a woman, and more specifically a Black woman, would be president of the United States one day. One could argue that hers is a glass cliff appointment, during COVID and after considerable political strife. Although she has not been hugely popular in her first term, her presence has made it easier for others to imagine a Black woman president and likely encouraged others to consider top political positions. Changes in images of leaders may encourage more Black women to visualize themselves in leadership positions and to seek these opportunities. Changing stereotypes might also lead others to nominate more Black women for executive-level positions.

Increasing numbers may also provide Black women leaders with a sense of community and provide space for authenticity. I deeply appreciate my network of Black women deans. Although we are at different types of institutions and we come from varied backgrounds, we share a set of experiences and understandings that transcend other boundaries. Norwood notes that a critical mass of Black women leaders could facilitate coalition-building, social support, and the development of shared material and initiatives. My informal relations with other Black women leaders support this view. I also belong to the Council of Black Education Deans, a group of about forty Black deans of education schools. We meet regularly to provide each other with social support and to foster a sense of community where we can openly discuss challenges and develop solutions. We engage around issues related to race (for example, "deaning while Black," recruiting diverse students and faculty) and those that are more generic (for example, appointing department chairs, improving enrollments). On occasion, we meet during or alongside other gatherings of deans as a way of making issues related to Black education more visible.

One of the best resources associated with membership is the roster, which I use regularly when I am looking for a listening ear or expert input on issues that I am facing. There is a strength that comes with numbers that may encourage retention in the role and lead to more lasting change. Black women leaders may also bring intellectual diversity to institutions, including perspectives from critical studies that are rooted in Black women's intellectual history. Black women are likely to engage in race-related scholarship, but they also can apply a critical lens to everything from tenure and promotion to strategic planning and recruitment of diverse student bodies.

Social and cultural events of the past decade have led to an increase in the numbers of Black women being called to lead in higher education. My hope is that these changes are not fleeting and superficial responses to institutional guilt over race and gender inequality but are substantive shifts in views about who can lead. If the trend continues, it may foster longevity and success for a new group of leaders.

THE GLASS CLIFF

Although there are likely many reasons for the increasing numbers of Black women leaders in some fields, one possibility is that many institutions are facing a range of crises, including economic uncertainty, racial strife, and political divisiveness, and they see Black women as skilled at leading during a crisis. There is growing evidence that women are more likely than men to be hired for leadership roles during times of organizational crisis, a situation termed the glass cliff (Ryan and Haslam). Initially, it was believed that women's leadership *caused* organizational challenges; that is, that women were poor leaders. However, follow-on research showed that women are more likely than men to be appointed during difficult times, perhaps because they are viewed as good leaders (Ryan et al., "Think Crisis, Think Female"). Morgenroth and colleagues conducted a meta-analysis of seventy-four studies of the glass cliff and found evidence that women are indeed more likely than men to be chosen to lead in times of trouble, that this effect is stronger in education and political fields than sports, and that the effect is stronger for Black women than for others.

The nation's racial crisis may have led to the increased hiring of Black women. In addition, their appointments may have resulted from gender disparities that were exacerbated by the COVID-19 pandemic (Fisher and Ryan). Given the timing of these increases, a cynical person might believe that hiring Black women would provide cover for universities facing criticism for racial and gender inequality, a superficial move that would suggest that the changes might be short-lived. In support of this hypothesis, one study found that companies that engaged in significant diversity-related hiring during the pandemic are phasing out those roles just a few years later (Bunn; Elias). Tiffany Cross, an MSNBC host hired during the pandemic and racial reckoning suggested that her firing reflected a return to "business as usual" after a superficial effort at change (Ellis). A more hopeful view would be that universities recognize the ability of Black women to be sensitive to the needs of marginalized faculty and students or a reflection of new efforts around inclusive leadership training (Lederman). Either way, Black women are being hired at record rates into positions with a high potential for failure or that will require great emotional and physical sacrifice.

One question that has not been well addressed is whether women hired into glass cliff positions are indeed more effective than others. These leaders sometimes face an uphill battle. Institutions in crisis are likely to be experiencing budget constraints and flagging morale. In glass cliff situations, leaders will often be asked to make sweeping changes, such as program closures or consolidations that might be unpopular. Moreover, institutions hiring Black women are often expecting them to do the impossible: effect structural change in the name of equity, but not disrupt long-standing power structures of the academy (Hodges and Welch). Still, there is the possibility that the confidence imparted to Black women leaders is well deserved. That is, Black women may indeed be great choices for institutions in crisis.

One example of women providing more effective leadership than men was in the case of responses to the COVID-19 pandemic where countries led by women experienced fewer COVID-related deaths (Fisher and Ryan). These leaders were clearly under tremendous pressure to lead effectively under precarious circumstances. Moreover, they seem to have succeeded at least in part because of characteristics that are stereotypic of women leaders—they were more likely to value human life over economic considerations.

The cliff, though, also implies a level of vulnerability. The crises at hand included the social upheaval, but also plummeting enrollments, rising dissatisfaction, a "great resignation," and financial distress. The Black women being hired were starting their positions remotely with few and shifting resources. Ryan and colleagues suggest that backlash in the face of women leaders' failures may be more swift and severe ("Getting on Top of the Glass Cliff"). Some Black women leaders became aware that they were expected to turn things around for a troubled organization and resigned after realizing that they would not be fully supported in the reform efforts that they were hired to undertake. Leslie Lokko, dean of the Spitzer School of Architecture at City College of New York, famously resigned in October 2020 after just ten months of service, claiming a "crippling workload and lack of empathy for Black women" (Wainwright). In her interview with a Guardian reporter, she described how George Floyd's murder and COVID-19 led to dramatic increases in her workload, budget cuts, and insufficient staff support. Lokko's hiring fits the picture of the glass cliff. The school was in crisis after not having had permanent leadership for four years.

Ryan and colleagues ("Getting on Top of the Glass Cliff") found some evidence that institutions are more open to risk-taking and experimentation during crises, a fact that may open up possibilities for innovation and change. However, Lokko noted that she experienced resistance to her initial efforts at change. Lokko was open about her commitments to DEI work during her interview and had imagined that she could apply some of the successes from her time as a leader at an institution in South Africa at Spitzer. She did not, however, experience uniform support for her efforts. My own experience suggests that universities sometimes have more of a commitment to demographic diversity than to real cultural diversity. They are eager to hire Black women as evidence of support for diversity efforts, but are not necessarily committed to enacting significant structural changes or to pushing for racial equity. As Carolyn Hodges, in her book with Olga Welch, notes in her description of her time as the only Black dean at her institution at the time and the first one in her position, colleagues are not always prepared to take up difficult topics or to engage in the introspection that might be necessary to move certain work forward. Hodges described the strategies that she used to bring her colleagues along on tough issues, but some leaders may find the burden of changing minds too difficult. Tone-setting from above could go a long way to achieving buy-in for Black women leaders.

Many institutions declared a commitment to racial justice in the wake of George Floyd's death, but their strategies most often took the form of hiring, observing the Juneteenth holiday, and the formation of book clubs or support groups. I suspect that few universities reviewed things like pay equity, recruitment practices, or efforts to raise visibility of the work of scholars of color. The hiring of Black women leaders may not move the needle on racial justice if Black women are not provided the resources to succeed, are handed insurmountable problems, or do not have the political support to enact meaningful change.

To summarize, we may be seeing the rise of more Black women leaders because of the glass cliff; women are more likely to be hired during times of crisis and we are facing several social, political, and health-related crises right now. At the same time, it is possible that the leaders will thrive, changing the face of higher education leadership going forward.

BLACK WOMEN PLAYING DUAL ROLES

The image of Black women as strong, selfless, nurturing, and subservient is at the intersection of race and gender stereotypes (Harris-Perry). Although there is little literature that directly speaks to this phenomenon, I imagine that Black women are viewed as effective leaders during crises because people believe that they will care for the community *and* that they can manage adversity well. When I am contacted by search firms who are working to fill top administrative posts, I always ask what the organization is looking for in a leader and why they think that I might be a good fit. In many cases, they say that they are looking for someone with my expertise in diversity, equity, and inclusion, or they cite the institution's need for healing after some type of trauma. My CV certainly includes evidence of my DEI commitments, including my serving as associate chair for diversity in the psychology department at the University of Michigan and awards that I have won from organizations that serve students of color. However, there is nothing, other than my being a Black woman, that would lead someone to assume that I was skilled at nurturing or healing distressed organizations. In one instance, the firm trying to fill the provost position at a research institution openly shared some of the challenges that the school had faced in recent years and suggested that I might be just the person who could bring about some healing. There was no mention of my experience as the associate vice president for research at the University of Michigan or my time leading the largest Psychology department in the country.

I came upon the notion of the administrative mammy role through an interaction with a colleague, another Black woman, at an institution where I was dean. I was initially taken aback by her characterization of me as a mammy. Mammy is a fictionalized character whose image was rooted in slavery. Mammies were Black women who were motherly and selfless in their service to the slave master and his family. This image was used to portray slaves as happy and loyal (Bell and Nkomo). I thought that by calling me a mammy, my colleague was suggesting that I was a pawn of my supervisors or that I lacked integrity in some way. However, after the meeting, she shared a decades-old book chapter by Rhetaugh Dumas called *The Dilemma of Black Females in Leadership*. In this chapter, Dumas provides an analysis of conversations with numerous Black women leaders that described how they are expected to nurture the community but also fulfill the core responsibilities related to their job (for example, managing the budget, recruitment and retention, enrollment). Dumas highlights the myth that Black women are both exceptionally strong and possess a "unique capacity for warm, soothing interpersonal interactions" (206)—mammies. They are torn between fulfilling the mythic role as mammy and the established role as traditional leader. In addition, as was the case in my encounter with my colleague, Black women leaders are asked to intervene in situations related to race and sex, especially when they involve the aggression of Black males or anger of Black females.

According to Dumas, the Black woman leader, as mythical mammy, is expected to lead with their interpersonal skills through informal systems. She must be willing to "put her person at the disposal of others" (207). To be sure, these responsibilities require sacrifice not asked of others, that is, to stand for equity and justice and provide support for marginalized groups. When I was dean at Teachers College, I was regularly asked by faculty and administrator colleagues to do things that my white male colleagues were not asked to do, such as to intervene on behalf of students of color. For example, during the COVID-19 lockdown, my coworkers asked me to go to the white men leaders and plead the case of our essential staff, who were mostly people of color and who did not have the option to work from home. One aspect of the dilemma is that Black women may have taken their role with the hopes that they could improve the experiences of marginalized people. Indeed, these moments were among the most meaningful of my time there, as I felt like I was making a difference for the community. However, I also recognized that these responsibilities required additional time—time that others did not have to sacrifice and time that would not "count" in my evaluations.

The mammy stereotype relates to what has been more recently termed the Strong Black Woman stereotype in some ways. As Dumas noted, many people view Black women as unusually strong, able to withstand physical and emotional hardship. The Black women that I know experience this stereotype with mixed feelings. It is hard not to feel proud of the legacy of Black women carrying their families when male partners were stripped away during slavery or because of high rates of incarceration in the Black community. The internet is filled with tributes to Black women, for example, as the group with the fastest rising college enrollments and as the most significant voting bloc of the Democratic party. As noted, I suspect that this stereotype explains some part of the recent round of hiring of Black women deans and presidents.

The consequences of the stereotype, however, can be complex. On the one hand, Black women are likely to endure adversity because they see themselves as strong and the stereotype reinforces perseverance. On the other hand, they are likely to pay a price for the stress and overwork that accompanies those accomplishments (West et al.). West and colleagues found that the young Black women that they interviewed felt good about their confidence and competence but were also aware of the harmful effects of the stress and perfectionism. Liao and colleagues found that endorsement of the Strong Black Woman schema by Black women resulted in maladaptive perfectionism, low self-compassion, and depressive symptoms. Given the probable crisis that prompted their hiring, Black women are also more likely to be working in an understaffed and underfunded context (Ellis). These leaders will be essentially taking on two jobs—the mythic and the traditional—and will be more likely to experience the negative effects in their physical and mental well-being. Dumas notes that playing the mammy role either takes time away from tasks associated with the traditional role or requires herculean efforts to accomplish both. In addition, these leaders will still be judged by the same criteria as their predecessors—research productivity, enrollments, and scholarly reputation (Dumas)—but their attention to these issues will be divided, with negative effects on success. Thus, Black women leaders who embrace expectations that they can be all things to all people, as in the mammy role, are likely to suffer significant negative consequences, and may, in fact, be less likely to succeed in their role.

These views of Black women as unusually strong may be especially damaging given evidence that Black women leaders often lack networking opportunities and role models (Reynolds-Dobbs et al.). When faced with challenges, Black women are less likely than others to have peers or mentors to be able to call on for support. Moreover, there is some evidence that women who embrace the stereotype will be less likely to seek help in difficult circumstances (Monterrosa).

If the Strong Black Woman stereotype is potentially damaging for Black women leaders, they might consider rejecting the stereotype. If Black women are seen as strong and selfless, rejection of the stereotype could include finding ways to distribute the workload, requesting additional resources, or refusing to shoulder the emotional needs of others. Counter-stereotypic behavior might be setting boundaries around work hours and accessibility or conserving one's energy by turning down additional service commitments. The dilemma here is that in glass cliff situations, these women were likely hired for previous demonstrations of strength and selflessness and may be faced with formidable challenges.

Black women who take on the traditional role and eschew the mythic roles of comforter and counselor will likely be viewed as less successful and less likable than others.

There are many stories of Black women leaders who have died during their tenures. My women of color friends and I read the story of Joanne Epps, interim president of Temple University, in horror. Just a few months after Dr. Epps stepped into the interim role, she died at a formal university event. Dr. Epps was carried off the stage after a medical episode and the event continued. Although we do not have information about Dr. Epps's health to that point or about the cause of her untimely death, many Black women saw the moment as a cautionary tale. In attempting to satisfy all of the expectations, we are sacrificing our health. Moreover, the machine that is higher education will continue to churn forward without us.

The dangers of these stereotypes are amplified right now because many of the current generation of Black women leaders are the first in their roles. I was not the first Black woman provost/dean at Teachers College, but I am for the University of Virginia Education School. The firstness of these roles puts additional pressure on Black women leaders to succeed. Some note a fear that their failure would decrease the likelihood that their organization would hire another Black woman in the future (2022). In their book, Hodges and Welch discussed their experiences as inaugural Black women deans. They discussed freely the challenges of meeting the expectations of their new colleagues. I was struck by the compassion with which they noted that their presence forced others to reimagine school leadership and, perhaps, to grieve perceived losses or fear the changes that were occurring and face their own discomfort with change.

In this section I laid out three dilemmas for Black women leaders. First, they are expected to serve as nurturers to their constituents, but also held to account for more traditional indicators of success. Second, they are symbols of institutional commitment to DEI, but often not able to enact system-level changes to diversity, equity, and inclusion. And third, the stereotypic strength that makes them attractive job candidates may also be their personal and professional undoing. Institutions must create the conditions to support the change that the leaders are being hired to enact, and the leaders themselves must find ways to set appropriate boundaries to protect against the consequences of hard work in the absence of adequate support.

INSTITUTIONAL SUPPORT FOR BLACK WOMEN LEADERS

To achieve the lasting changes that universities often seek, their commitments to diversifying leadership cannot end at hiring. Supporting Black women leaders can go a long way to improving the diversity of faculty, staff, and students, and increasing feelings of belonging and empowerment for all. Their failure may have a chilling effect on institutional commitment to diversity or serve as an indication of the extent to which people of color will be included.

The commitment to the success of a Black woman leader should start with the announcement of her appointment. University communications can remind constituents of the full range of expertise that the leader brings. The institution must consider the impact of emphasizing the race and gender of the individual. When I was named dean at UVA, a news reporter asked me how I felt about being the first Black woman (and actually the first person not a white man) to lead the school. Though I was obviously aware of this fact, I was not interested in highlighting my status as "other" as I started a new job. I also wanted to avoid being described as inspirational or as having a special mandate given my race and gender. I had hoped for a full discussion of my qualifications for the position, including my expertise in developing just and equitable organizations. Unfortunately, the story that the reporter published limited her comments to my race and gender and my DEI-related goals.

The initial days of an appointment may be especially important in shaping the sense of belonging for Black women leaders. Having the opportunity to meet other women leaders or leaders of color might help them feel connected. These networking opportunities, one of the activities that Liao and colleagues call collective coping, can reduce negative mental health and loneliness outcomes for Black women leaders. They may also facilitate future help-seeking.

Performance expectations will also be critical for the success of Black women leaders. Universities must acknowledge that Black women leaders will likely experience increased workload by virtue of their race and gender. There can be tremendous benefit in Black women's ability to connect with marginalized members of the community in terms of overall productivity and social climate. These efforts should be recognized in evaluation systems for all leaders, given the importance of inclusion and because these additional responsibilities may affect Black women's ability to address other issues. Institutional values and rewards for these efforts should be articulated up front so that leaders can make conscious choices about their time and make visible the hidden labor that has caused Black women leaders in higher education and industry to step away from their jobs (Ellis).

Once expectations are clear, universities also owe it to the candidate to protect against glass cliff catastrophe, either by offering the resources needed to address the crisis or by adjusting definitions of success to match the resources that are available. For example, timetables for deliverables should reflect staffing shortages, budget shortfalls, and "clean-up" work that must be done before the core issues can be addressed. Finally, if universities are hiring Black women to lead change, they must create the various conditions needed to allow for it. They must pave the way for systemic change, preferably through well-articulated strategic plans and public statements. They must also provide adequate mentoring and coaching to help the leaders to develop a plan to manage change effectively.

ADVICE FOR BLACK WOMEN LEADERS

Make no mistake, Black women leaders are deserving of the opportunities in front of them. Their identification as potential change agents, community builders, and transformative leaders is well deserved because Black women have always had to identify creative approaches to their work. Thus, my first piece of advice is to embrace the confidence of others and accept the challenges. Of course, this enthusiasm must be tempered somewhat to also reflect the complexities outlined in this chapter.

Although I framed the tensions between a traditional leadership role and DEI work as a conundrum, it need not be. At a luncheon for women of color faculty at the University of Michigan with Dr. Ruth Simmons, then president of Brown University, Dr. Simmons suggested that we not run from our race and gender, from specializing in ethnic or gender studies, or from leading diversity-related efforts. Rather, she encouraged us to engage in this work if it is where our passions lie, but to make sure that we have the resources needed to do excellent work. As I noted earlier, my work with faculty, staff, and students of color has been incredibly meaningful for me and I would enjoy my job less if I were not able to do it. Dr. Simmons also encouraged us to garner resources for the causes that are most important to us and to be keenly focused on their success. It is important, though, to understand where these activities fall in the university's reward system and make conscious choices about where to spend time.

I recommend that leaders of any background clarify and articulate their leadership goals and values. These goals and values should inform which opportunities are pursued but also how leaders show up in the new setting. Clear goals and values will foster intentional engagements and avoid the instinct to try to be all things to all people. If the reluctant understand the logic being applied, they may be more patient during the change process. In addition, careful advance planning and regular progress review can help leaders to monitor progress toward equity-focused goals as well as traditional indicators. In my view, intentional leadership is the only way to take on both roles without completely sacrificing well-being.

One challenge for leaders is to discern the difference between a risky but well-fitting challenge and a sinking ship. Before taking on a leadership role, candidates must ask difficult questions about the resources available and the criteria for evaluation. Where possible, it is important to negotiate for the resources that one needs to make required improvements. Candidates should also pay close attention to the experiences of other leaders and whether they report feeling well-supported. In short, taking on a leadership role may be incredibly gratifying. Effective mentoring, explicit support, and advance vetting of the position can prepare Black women leaders for high-impact roles.

CONCLUSION

The ascension of a significant number of Black women to leadership positions in corporate America and higher education is cause for cautious celebration. Though the COVID-19 pandemic and racial reckoning brought new enthusiasm for Black women leaders in some fields, Black women are still dramatically underrepresented in academe generally and among academic leaders overall (Lewis-Strickland). Moreover, even with increasing numbers, Black women leaders still face the same challenges that led to their underrepresentation (Lewis-Strickland). Still, just as the inauguration of Barack Obama as America's first Black president was met with jubilation in the Black community and beyond, we are celebrating the Black women who have reached the highest positions. These women are charting new territory, opening new doors, and changing the culture of higher education. Their visibility and commitment to diversity and inclusion will likely increase opportunities for students, faculty, and staff of color in predominantly white institutions.

I also imagine that the sense of a critical mass will help these leaders to persevere during difficult times and spur innovation. My hope is that this is the beginning of a new trend, rather than a flash in the pan.

AUTHOR'S NOTE

In the time since the writing of this chapter, the country has seen considerable backlash against DEI in higher education and corporate America, the ouster of President Gay and other women presidents of Ivy League universities, and Vice President Kamala Harris's unsuccessful bid for president. It remains to be seen how these events will change the experiences of Black women leaders.

WORKS CITED

Amponsah, Peter, and Juanita Stephen. "Developing a Practice of African-Centred Solidarity in Child and Youth Care." *International Journal of Child, Youth and Family Studies*, vol. 11, no. 2, 2020, pp. 6–24.

Bell, Ella L. J., and Stella M. Nkomo. Our Separate Ways: Black and White Women and the Struggle for Professional Identity. *Harvard Business Review Press*, 2001.

Bunn, Curtis. "Hamstrung by 'Golden Handcuffs': Diversity Roles Disappear Three Years After George Floyd's Murder Inspired Them." *NBC News*, 27 Feb. 2023, https://www.nbcnews.com/news/nbcblk/diversity-roles-disappear-three-years-george-floyd-protests-inspired-rcna72026.

Dumas, Rhetaugh Graves. "Dilemmas of Black Females in Leadership." *The Black Woman*, edited by La Frances Rodgers-Rose, Sage Publications, 1980, pp. 203–15.

Elias, Jennifer. "Tech Companies Like Google and Meta Made Cuts to DEI after Big Promises in Prior Years." *CNBC*, 22 Dec. 2023, https://www.cnbc.

com/2023/12/22/google-meta-other-tech-giants-cut-dei-programs
-in-2023.html?taid=65859a3151a48f0001c18201&utm_campaign=true
anthem&utm_medium=social&utm_source=twitter%7Cmain.

Ellis, Nicquel Terry. "'Very Rarely Is It as Good as It Seems': Black Women
in Leadership Are Finding Themselves on the 'Glass Cliff.'" *CNN*, 17 Dec.
2022, https://www.cnn.com/2022/12/17/us/black-women-glass-cliff-reaj
/index.html.

Fisher, Alexandra N., and Michelle K. Ryan. "Gender Inequalities During
COVID-19." *Group Processes & Intergroup Relations*, vol. 24, no. 2, 2021,
pp. 237–45.

Harold, Erika, and Julia Roundtree Livingston. "Meet the Black Women Leading Illinois Law Schools." *2 Civility*, 23 Feb. 2023, https://www.2civility
.org/black-women-law-deans-illinois-law-schools.

Harris-Perry, Melissa V. *Sister Citizen: Shame, Stereotypes, and Black Women
in America*. Yale UP, 2011.

Hodges, Carolyn, and Olga Welch. *Truth Without Tears: African American Women Deans Share Lessons in Leadership*. Harvard Education Press,
2018.

Lederman, Doug. "Diversity on the Rise Among College Presidents." *Inside
Higher Education*, 13 Feb. 2022, https://www.insidehighered.com
/news/2022/02/14/colleges-have-hired-more-minority-presidents-amid
-racial-reckoning.

Lewis-Strickland, Kendra. "Advice From a Seat at the Table: Exploring
the Leadership Resilience Development of Black Women University
Deans." *Journal of Higher Education Policy and Leadership Studies*, vol. 2,
no. 1, 2021, pp. 29–43.

Liao, Kelly Yu-Hsin, et al. "The Misunderstood Schema of the Strong
Black Woman: Exploring Its Mental Health Consequences and
Coping Responses Among African American Women." *Psychology of Women Quarterly*, vol. 44, no. 1, 2020, pp. 84–104, https://doi.
org/10.1177/0361684319883198.

Monterrosa, Allison E. "How Race and Gender Stereotypes Influence Help-

Seeking for Intimate Partner Violence." *Journal of Interpersonal Violence*, vol. 36, nos. 17–18, 2021. *Sage Journals*, https://doi.org/10.1177/0886260519 853403.

Morgenroth, Thekla, et al. "The Who, When, and Why of The Glass Cliff Phenomenon: A Meta-Analysis of Appointments to Precarious Leadership Positions." *Psychological Bulletin*, vol. 146, no. 9, 2020, pp. 797–829.

Norwood, Candice. "More Black Women Are Leading U.S. Law Schools and Changing the Conversation on Race and Gender." *The 19th*, 8 Feb. 2022, https://19thnews.org/2022/02/black-women-law-school-deans/.

Reynolds-Dobbs, Wendy, et al. "From Mammy to Superwoman: Images That Hinder Black Women's Career Development." *Journal of Career Development*, vol. 35, no. 2, Dec. 2008, pp. 129–50.

Ryan, Michelle K., et al. "Think Crisis–Think Female: The Glass Cliff and Contextual Variation in the Think Manager–Think Male Stereotype." *Journal of Applied Psychology*, vol. 96, no. 3, 2011, pp. 470–84.

Ryan, Michelle K., and S. Alexander Haslam. "The Glass Cliff: Evidence that Women Are Over-Represented in Precarious Leadership Positions." *British Journal of Management*, vol. 16, no. 2, 2005, pp. 81–90.

Ryan, Michelle K., et al. "Getting on Top of the Glass Cliff: Reviewing a Decade of Evidence, Explanations, and Impact." *The Leadership Quarterly*, vol. 27, no. 3, 2016, pp. 446–55.

Spanierman, Lisa B. "Confronting Whiteness in Developmental Science: Disrupting the Intergenerational Transmission of White Racism." *Journal of Research on Adolescence*, vol. 32, no. 3, 2022, pp. 808–14.

Thompson, Ife. "An Introduction to Anti-Racism Lawyering." Howard League for Penal Reform, https://howardleague.org/wp-content/uploads/2020/07/Anti-Racism-Legal-slides-by-Ife-Thompson-.pdf.

Wainwright, Oliver. "'Race Is Never Far from the Surface': Lesley Lokko on Quitting New York." *The Guardian*, 20 Oct. 2020, https://www.theguardian.com/artanddesign/2020/oct/20/lesley-lokko-quit-new-york-spitzer-architecture.

West, Lindsey M., et al. "The Price of Strength: Black College Women's

Perspectives on the Strong Black Woman Stereotype." *Women & Therapy*, vol. 39, nos. 3–4, 2016, pp. 390–412.

3

THE REASON UNIVERSITIES DON'T HAVE MORE BLACK WOMEN IN HIGHER EDUCATION ACADEMIC LEADERSHIP IS BECAUSE THEY DON'T WANT THEM!

Revisiting the Past to Reshape the Present

WANDA J. BLANCHETT

THE ORIGINS OF AMERICAN HIGHER EDUCATION

To understand more fully the reason universities, and specifically predominantly white institutions (PWIs), do not have more Black women leaders, one must examine the history of higher education in the United States, that is, whom the American higher education system was designed to serve and why. To be sure, what is currently known as the higher education system in the United States has a history that goes back to the 1600s and long before the founding of the United States of America in 1776 (Attridge). Attridge asserts,

> In 1636, only a handful of years after British settlers established their
> first permanent colonies on the coast of North America, Harvard

College began educating students. For over 300 years, Harvard admitted only white men from prominent families—that is, until the 19th century, when women turned the tide in their fight for a place at America's universities.

Harvard College graduated its first class of nine students in 1642, and this inaugural class consisted only of Christian white men (History of Privilege). Accordingly, discrimination, racism, white male privilege, and elitism were engrained into what would become the American higher education system from the very beginning. "Harvard reinforced the exclusive nature of higher education by not ranking its graduates by their grades or alphabetically … [instead they] crossed the stage according to the rank their families held in society" (History of Privilege).

In his review of J. David Hoeveler's *Creating the American Mind: Intellect and Politics in the Colonial Colleges*, Howard Miller points to the successful attempts of colonial Americans at "institution building," namely of the nine original colonial colleges that to this day are lauded as elite institutions: "Harvard, William and Mary, Yale, the College of New Jersey (Princeton), King's College (Columbia), the College of Philadelphia (the University of Pennsylvania), the College of Rhode Island (Brown), Queen's College (Rutgers), and Dartmouth," which are all in New England and parts of the Northeast (1553). Admission to these denominational colleges would remain open only to the most elite white Christian men from prominent families for over three hundred years (History of Privilege). Accordingly, poor and working-class white men, along with white women, and Black women and men were all denied admission to these and other colleges that were established exclusively for white elite Christian men for hundreds of years to ensure that the nation had a learned clergy and informed politicians. As sad as this historical context regarding the American higher education system is, every element of progress that has been achieved in this country toward extending educational and voting rights and privileges to Black and other people of color and to white women has only been achieved through resistance/ protest and litigation followed by legislation (Blanchett and Zion).

While we are not where we need to be regarding access to higher education and academic leadership on many fronts for historically excluded and often marginalized communities in the academy, considerable progress has been made for white women. However, Black women and Black men still do not enjoy the same nurturing or comparable advancement opportunities as their white counterparts. I contend that many of the barriers and challenges that Black women experience in trying to scale, and prevail on the academic ladder are an inherent part of the higher education culture in this country that has been present since its beginnings. Hence, it should not come as a surprise that much of the racism, sexism, hegemony, elitism, white privilege, and anti-Blackness that served as the foundation for the establishment of the American higher education system is still very much at work in today's predominantly white institutions of higher education.

THE LONG ROAD TOWARD ACCESS AND DIVERSITY IN THE AMERICAN HIGHER EDUCATION SYSTEM

Though institutions of higher education were formed in the 1600s, the first Black person recorded to have attended a US college would not come until 1799 in the person of John Chavis, a Presbyterian minister, yet there is no written record of his graduation from what is now Washington and Lee University ("JBHE Chronology" 77). Alexander Lucius Twilight was the first Black person known to graduate from a US college when he earned a bachelor's degree from Middlebury College in Vermont in 1823 ("JBHE Chronology" 77). Dartmouth College appears to be the first of the original colonial colleges to graduate a Black student—Edward Mitchell—in 1828. During this time period, a number of denominations began to open more colleges, including the founding of Oberlin College in 1833 by Presbyterians in Ohio. Oberlin adopted a then ground-breaking and progressive stance with the decision shortly after its founding to admit all people regardless of race, making it the first integrated and coeducational college in America ("JBHE Chronology" 77). Higher education access for Black Americans grew with the establishment of the African Institute, which would later change to the Institute for Colored Youth in 1837 and, finally, to Cheyney University in Pennsylvania for the education of free Black people in agriculture and trades (Patterson; "JBHE Chronology" 77). In 1844 Oberlin graduated its first Black student, George B. Vashon, who would become one of the founding professors of Howard University.

Despite progress being made with regard to Black students' higher education access in the United States, Harvard did not admit its first Black undergraduate student until 1847, who sadly died and never matriculated. Wilberforce University, the second Historically Black College, was founded in Ohio in 1856. Martin Henry Freeman became President of Avery College in 1856 and also the first Black college president in the United States. This means that from the founding of America's first college, Harvard College, in 1636 to the appointment of President Freeman as America's first Black college president, it would take literally 220 years. In 1850, Harvard admitted its first three Black students to Harvard Medical School but yielded to white students' resistance and rescinded their admission. Though a few Black men were granted access to higher education in Europe and in the US, Black and white women were still largely denied admission. In fact, it was not until 1862 that Oberlin College conferred a bachelor's degree on Mary Jane Patterson, making her the first Black woman to earn a college degree in the US. However, access to America's most elite colleges would take even longer. Harvard would eventually admit another Black undergraduate student, Richard Theodore Greener, who graduated in 1870, which was 228 years after Harvard graduated its first class of white men ("JBHE Chronology").

Thus, with few exceptions, our higher education system has too long stayed true to its original intent, which was to deny admission to anyone who was not an elite white Christian man. In the 1860s, Sophia Jex-Blake sought admission to Harvard College and was denied admission because there was "no provision for the education of women in any department of the university" (History of Privilege). Though Jex-Blake and several other women were granted admission to Edinburgh University in Scotland, they were assessed greater fees than the admitted men, and the men on the faculty had the university's support not to teach them. Most importantly, "the university refused to grant degrees to any of the seven women. Institutional barriers, such as universities denying admission to women or allowing faculty to refuse to teach women students, created nearly insurmountable barriers to higher education, which was designed to protect the privilege of students who saw college as their domain and theirs alone" (History of Privilege).

As Attridge illustrated, it took so long to integrate American higher education because its protectors were determined to preserve admission for those privileged few whom they deemed to be deserving of access, and they had no intention of becoming more inclusive or diverse with regard to admitting Black students or white women. In summary, early American institutions of higher education were not integrated on purpose because they did not want to be. In fact, those with money, including religious denominations, were willing to use their funds to build separate institutions of higher education for Black people and women to avoid having to admit them to their white male institutions. Similarly, when I look at the disturbing lack of Black women in top academic leadership positions, I have to conclude that the reason these elite universities do not have more Black women in those roles is simply because "they don't want them" in the academy at all, let alone to hold those leadership positions. One only has to look at how few Black women and women of color have achieved the rank of full professor at many research institutions in comparison with their white peers. Additionally, while white men and women have been known to move into academic leadership positions without having successfully matriculated through the faculty ranks, rarely are Black faculty successful in doing the same. Thus, we have to work intentionally and diligently to encourage and assist Black women in achieving the rank of full professor, so that they can reasonably consider and aspire to leadership opportunities that enable them to break through the "concrete ceiling."

INSTITUTIONAL BARRIERS AND BROKEN PATHWAYS TO ACADEMIC LEADERSHIP FOR BLACK WOMEN

Even with some of the encouraging progress noted previously, the institutional barriers that Black women have encountered in trying to access higher education over several centuries still exist at many levels, albeit in different forms. The barriers that they confront today are in many instances not as blatant as they once were; however, they are nonetheless as exclusionary and damaging to the careers of these women. Along with roadblocks they encounter in the academy, such as having their credentials questioned more than their white peers, being asked to take on service roles that are work-heavy and time-consuming and detract from their focus on research, and dealing with surroundings and policies that ignore accommodations to support personal and familial needs, Black women face additional challenges in the workplace that hamper their progress. These challenges include minimal mentoring and sponsorship to support their research agendas, research funding pursuits, and professional development activities that require financial support, such as conference participation and attending special seminars and workshops.

Because many of them often carry a large service load when it comes to student advising or serving as advisors to student diversity support organizations, Black women faculty tend to have a heavier service workload than their peers. Accordingly, their service workload can negatively impact their ability to conduct the volume of research required for professorial promotion through the ranks. Because Black women faculty's important contributions to service are not viewed as strong contributing factors in their bid for promotion, it is often invisible work and not viewed positively with respect to their promotion. Additionally, Black women often become designated as the authentic voice of reason and advice for many, if not all, of the Black students in a department or student organization, not because there is a reasonable principle for that idea nor because the Black faculty member requested that designation but because it relieves the white faculty of the obligation. This approach sets up a stereotypical view of the Black students and the Black faculty member (about who can relate to whom based on race), when, in fact, students are all simply looking for attention, support, and guidance from whoever delivers it, regardless of race or gender. Just because many Black faculty care deeply about all students and can relate to students from diverse backgrounds does not justify scapegoating them in this way and releasing often more senior white faculty from their responsibilities to contribute to providing an ethic of care for all students and to mentor both students and new faculty.

Most importantly, even today Black women often find themselves as either the only one or one of only two to three women of color in their program or department and sometimes the whole school. Furthermore, if they do succeed in getting on the path to leadership in administration, they are often the "first" and must struggle to find trustworthy support. The feeling of isolation is real as they watch their white colleagues being invited to informal gatherings—be it to lunch, dinner, or scheduled meetings of select groups to which they are not invited—at which information about special opportunities for advancement is shared or they are nominated for awards and recognized for their work on campus, inside and outside the classroom as well as their external activities that bring positive attention and prestige to their institution.

As a result, Black women become visibly invisible: visible because they represent the diversity the institution wants to claim but invisible because they are not included in the day-to-day collegial interactions. In the case of one particularly unsettling example, I recently learned that although an exceptional Black woman faculty member had been in her department for three years after being hired during the pandemic, there were faculty members in that department who were unaware she was there as their faculty colleague. All new faculty and staff hires were introduced to the community and their appointments well-publicized, so there was no reasonable justification for anyone in the department to not be aware of her presence or her appointment as a faculty member. Yet, this really happened to an extraordinarily productive Black woman faculty member. Such a circumstance is particularly disturbing, as it represents the kind of blatant invisibility—not being acknowledged or seen by your white colleagues as a peer—that is very hard to accept, especially when you are exceeding the research and external funding expectations in terms of the quantity, quality, and prestige of your scholarship, teaching, and service. Most importantly, this is an example of the kinds of micro- and macro-aggressions that cause Black women in the academy physical, emotional, and psychological trauma, which drives them to seek employment at another institution or to leave the profession altogether.

When Black and other women of color conduct research on topics such as race, diversity, equity, inclusion, and other systemic issues related to racial and social justice as it relates to their disciplines, their research topics/agendas may not be viewed as legitimate or rigorous by their colleagues, department chairs, and others who are charged with evaluating their progress toward tenure and/or promotion. In addition, Black women often witness the discouraging treatment of Black women who are already in leadership, specifically by some white men who wield their privilege in their interactions with Black women leaders with reckless abandon with few, if any, senior white faculty holding them accountable. Even more importantly, Black women faculty often have to watch senior white women and men faculty with more status and social capital choose to not challenge their white peers for their disrespectful and sometimes blatantly racist and sexist actions. In the meantime, many Black women faculty remain silent due to not being tenured and the fact that they will indeed need the votes of some of those wielding their power when they seek promotion. When I entered the academy, I decided that regardless of my status and lack of power in the academy as an untenured assistant professor, in the words of Dr. Martin Luther King, Jr., "injustice anywhere is a threat to justice everywhere," so as a Black woman, I could not wait until I was tenured or a full professor to call out injustice as the only non-white faculty member in my department. This was because I was sure that if I did not call it out, there may never be another me. These kinds of experiences suggest that the reason we don't have more Black women in academic and administrative leadership at PWIs is because they are overlooked or they are not motivated to pursue leadership positions, fearing they will encounter this kind of negative treatment.

One of the signs that PWIs do not make concerted efforts to welcome Black women into academic leadership is the lack of Black and women of color who have achieved the rank of full professor. The inability to obtain promotion to the rank of full professor with tenure, in and of itself, is also one of the most significant barriers to Black and other women of color gaining access to top academic and administrative leadership positions at universities, including intermediary levels, such as department head or assistant/associate dean. The recent AAUW data (Silbert et al., "Elite Universities") suggest that seventy-three percent of tenured full professors are men, with men of color making up sixteen percent, and women making up twenty-seven percent, with women of color representing only six percent. As mentioned previously, while there are various pathways that one might take to move up the academic leadership ladder, for most, being an academic dean is the initial, most foundational step, and lacking experience at this level, especially as a woman, and specifically a Black woman, will not serve you well. At the rank of academic dean, sixty-one percent were men, of whom men of color comprised fourteen percent, while women made up thirty-nine percent of academic deans with women of color representing only eight percent. At the provost rank, sixty-two percent were men, with men of color representing only eight percent, and women represented thirty-eight percent, with women of color counting for just six percent. At the level of president, men accounted for seventy-eight percent of all presidents and men of color represented eighteen percent, while women made up twenty-two percent and women of color only five percent. At the level of system president, men represented ninety percent and men of color made up twelve percent; women comprised ten percent and women of color zero. The percentages of Black women and other women of color at every rank from full professors with tenure to system president are both revealing and troubling.

REIMAGINING ACADEMIC LEADERSHIP AT PWIS: INCREASING THE NUMBER OF BLACK AND OTHER WOMEN IN TOP LEADERSHIP POSITIONS

Given that the pathway to presidency for most women and people of color regardless of gender is typically one that requires having served as a provost or chief academic officer, the AAUW's recent finding that half of the presidents in their study reported having been provosts prior to ascending to the presidency is not surprising (Silbert et al., "Research Universities," 3). However, the AAUW concluded that since thirty-nine percent of provosts at elite institutions were women and thirty percent of presidents were women, there is "not a pipeline problem" (3). In reflecting on the progress made by white women with regard to their significant increase in presidencies at research universities, Silbert et al. concluded that "our data suggests that with increased awareness and bold, intentional effort, we can accelerate the progress toward diversity atop the Ivory Tower" ("Research Universities," 2). However, I would challenge that argument, as Black women are rarely appointed to provost at PWIs and many of these universities in 2024 have never had a Black woman or woman of color as provost or president. I contend instead that the pipeline for Black women and other historically underrepresented women and men with respect to appointments as presidents and provosts is indeed broken. And it is not just broken, but seemingly is broken beyond repair. The AAUW's 2023 Women's Power Gap report clearly articulated that there is a serious diversity gap and lag when it comes to Black women securing presidencies at the country's research universities. When the data are disaggregated, the small number of Black and Hispanic women at the level of the presidency is striking (Silbert et al., "Elite Universities"). As Johnnetta Cole, an outstanding Black scholar and leader who served as a former president of Bennett College and first woman president of Spelman College fittingly stated, "We must back up our belief in our ability to reinvent the academy by carrying out concrete actions to do so. There will be no more credit for predicting the rain. It's time to build the arks" (17). Accordingly, if we want more Black and women of color to scale the academic ladder and crack the concrete ceiling of executive academic and administrative leadership positions at research universities, we have to build the pathways for them. The recent and surging progress of white women in academic and administrative leadership at PWIs illustrates that when we are intentional and deliberate in providing the resources and opportunities for change, we are successful.

To begin to reimagine higher education academic leadership with the goal of increasing the number of Black women in academic leadership we need to do the following:

1. We must admit that given that the American higher education system was never designed with the intent or purpose to serve any woman or person of color, it is likely that many vestiges of

that exclusionary culture and practice still exist in most institutions of higher education today and must be disrupted and rebuilt with diversity, equity, and inclusion for **ALL** at the forefront.

2. We must continue to work toward changing the culture of higher education and both its institutional and organizational practices and policies to make them more inclusive, affirming, and supportive of the needs of all in the academy, especially Black women, and not just the privileged few. This also requires providing ongoing professional development for all faculty and staff so that they feel empowered both to speak up and to take appropriate action when needed. The culture of higher education must also hold those faculty and staff accountable who create a discriminatory and exclusionary culture by adopting policies that do not privilege research, external funding, and productivity over common decency and basic respect for all.

3. We must be intentional and deliberate in getting Black women to pursue careers as faculty at the country's PWIs. To do this, it is critical to provide Black women with the resources afforded their white peers (that is, reduced teaching loads, start-up research funds, summer research salaries, nominations for prestigious internal and external awards, and encouragement of participation in emerging leader programs), especially in disciplines where they are not represented at all or are significantly underrepresented. Otherwise, diligent efforts to increase their representation on the faculty leave no pathway for growth and end by stifling future opportunities.

4. We need to establish more doctoral and post-doctoral fellowship programs that are designed to recruit, prepare, retain, and support Black women for faculty positions, not only at high research universities, but also at the broad range of PWIs, small and large, public and private. Such a strategy places emphasis on including built-in support networks and ongoing professional development

for graduate students preparing for careers in academia.

5. We must develop leadership preparation, support, and advancement networks designed explicitly for Black women. History has demonstrated that being deliberate and intentional in this area can and does work as it is working for our white women. That kind of laser is critical for Black women if we are going to increase their representation among the top leaders in higher education.

We have a serious dilemma with regard to Black women's ability to scale the "concrete ceiling" of academic leadership and a lot of ground to make up. But the problem is not a lack of motivation, talent, or desire. The pipeline is indeed broken for Black women. However, from my perspective, the biggest challenge is the fact that PWIs are not willing or motivated to change the ways they have operated, preferring to rely on the status quo. Continuing to do what we always have done all too often leads to disappointment and, in extreme cases, disaster. There are amazing Black women in academia who are privileged to work with supportive and collegial leaders. On the other hand, there are tough Black women leaders who do not fare as well because they answer to leaders who are annoyed and, in many cases, threatened, not only by the strong capability of these women, but also by their willingness to speak out against inappropriate behaviors, by their determination to take corrective action rather than leaning on what has always been done, and by their dogged grip on integrity, which has no price.

One only has to look at two Black women leaders who are examples of the dilemma. Claudine Gay scaled the Ivory Tower of one of the country's most elite institutions of higher education to become the first Black person to ever lead Harvard University; sadly, we watched in dismay as she was toppled from that tower, lost her institutional support, and resigned in the interest of the institution (Habeshian). Shortly after that we learned about the shocking story of Antoinette "Bonnie" Candia-Bailey, who was the vice president for student affairs at her alma mater, Lincoln

University, a Historically Black College in Columbia, Missouri. After having requested a leave of absence to address her mental health issues and having reported her mistreatment by her supervisor to the University's Board, she reportedly was fired and tragically committed suicide that same day (Adams; Bryant). While we do not know all of the facts in either of these situations, we do know that these two Black women's attempts to serve in higher education senior leadership, albeit each in very different situations and with very different responsibilities, cost them dearly, yet they stood by the truth and were unwilling to relinquish their integrity. In order to transcend the barriers Black women leaders have faced, it is our duty to relinquish the lingering past errors of our ways and envision a future where we must do better!

WORKS CITED

Adams, Char. "Supporters Say Black Academic's Suicide Was Fueled by the Very Pressures She Studied in Her Dissertation." *NBC News*, 19 Jan. 2020, https://www.nbcnews.com/news/nbcblk/antoinette-bonnie-candida-bailey-lincoln-university-dissertation-rcna134380.

Attridge, Margaret. "A History of Women in Higher Education." *Best Colleges*, 20 Mar. 2023, https://www.bestcolleges.com/news/analysis/2021/03/21/history-women-higher-education/.

Blanchett, Wanda J., and Shelley D. Zion. "Black Youth Activism Was Pivotal to the Civil Right Movement: How Black Lives Matter Is Inspiring Education Activists of Today." *Young People Shaping Democratic Politics: Interrogating Inclusion, Mobilising Education*, edited by Ian Rivers and C. Laura Lovin, Palgrave Macmillan Cham, 2023, pp. 9–30.

Bryant, Jessica. "Lincoln University President on Paid Leave after Death of VP of Student Affairs." *Best Colleges*, 19 Jan. 2023, https://www.bestcolleges.com/news/lincoln-university-president-on-paid-leave-after-death-of-vp.

Cole, J. "Transcending Boundaries to Build a New Academic Leadership." *The*

Presidency, vol. 8, no. 1, 2005, pp. 14–19.

"Fast Facts: Women of Color in Higher Ed." American Association of University Women, https://www.aauw.org/resources/article/fast-facts-woc-higher-ed/. Accessed 18 Oct. 2022.

Habeshian, S. "How One Hearing Brought Down Two Ivy League Presidents." *Axios*, 2 Jan. 2024, https://www.axios.com/2024/01/02/ivy-league-presidents-antisemitism-hearings.

Harris, Michael S. "Historical Context of Institutional Diversity." *Understanding Institutional Diversity in American Higher Education, ASHE Higher Education Report*, 1st ed., Jossey-Bass, 2013, pp. 17–35.

"A History of Privilege in American Higher Education." *Best Colleges*, 16 Dec. 2021, https://www.bestcolleges.com/news/analysis/2020/07/17/history-privilege-higher-education/.

"JBHE Chronology of Major Landmarks in the Progress of African Americans in Higher Education." *Journal of Blacks in Higher Education*, no. 53, autumn 2006, pp. 77–88, http://www.jstor.org/stable/25073540.

King, Jr., Martin Luther. "Letter from Birmingham Jail." 16 Apr. 1963, https://www.africa.upenn.eduArticles_Birmingham.html.

Miller, Howard. Review of *Creating the American Mind: Intellect and Politics in the Colonial Colleges*, by J. David Hoeveler. *The American Historical Review*, vol. 109, no. 5, 2004, pp. 1553–54.

Patterson, Vanessa Leanne. "Cheyney University of Pennsylvania (1837–)." *BlackPast*, 6 July 2010, https://www.blackpast.org/african-american-history/cheyney-university-pennsylvania-1837/.

Silbert, Andrea, et al. "The Women's Power Gap at Elite Universities: Scaling the Ivory Tower." *The Women's Power Gap Study Series*, Eos Foundation, Jan. 2022, https://www.aauw.org/app/uploads/2022/01/WPG-Power-Gap-at-Elite-Universities-Full-Report.pdf.

Silbert, Andrea, et al. "The Women's Power Gap at Top Research Universities: 2021–2023 Progress Report." *The Women's Power Gap Study Series*, EoS Foundation, 2023, https://www.womenspowergap.org/wp-content/uploads/2023/05/WPG-R1-Progress-Report-2023.pdf.

4

FROM GATEKEEPING TO GROUNDSKEEPING

Cultivating Seeds of Black Women Emerging Leaders

TAM'RA-KAY FRANCIS

A t the sixty-sixth Grammy Awards, veteran multiplatinum singer-
songwriter Tracy Chapman returned to the stage to perform her
award-winning 1988 single "Fast Car" alongside country music superstar Luke Combs. Their duet was one of the most viewed per-
formances of the night, and, for many, one of the best for the show in
decades. People raved about the showstopping performance all night.
Post performance, Chapman's original version exploded in digital sales
and streams and entered the daily US Spotify and iTunes charts, with
the song, music video, and album taking the number one spot on iTunes.

It is important to note the significance of Chapman's surprise (re)ap-
pearance. Since releasing her last album in 2008 and touring in 2009,
she has kept a relatively low profile in the music world. This was the
four-time Grammy Award winner's first TV performance since 2015 on
the Late Show with David Letterman. Even after Combs's crossover,
"Fast Car," peaked at number two on the Billboard charts and Chapman
became the first Black person and songwriter to win the Country Music
Association's Song of the Year award, she remained out of the limelight.
But in one night, her reemergence bridged generations in ways like no

other. If you didn't know who Tracy Chapman was before that performance, you certainly did at that point.

Separate from the stellar performance, a discussion emerged among the Black community about how happy and beautiful Chapman seemed. On #BlackTwitter, Black women especially referenced the glow of her skin, her broad smile, the peace that seemed to encapsulate Chapman, and how emotional the performance was for them. Even now, in writing what had transpired, my eyes swell with tears with memories of my childhood. Chapman's self-titled debut was one of the first albums I could sing from start to finish, word for word. Something, however, was different this time, at least for most of us. I believe in that moment Chapman's joyful state represented the place where so many of us wanted to be—a liberatory space where we have nothing to prove. Chapman's brief appearance reminded many of us that even in restrictive spaces, we get to decide what joy looks like for us.

I cannot begin to count the number of times I paused and asked myself if I was the right person to speak about leadership development for the next generation of Black women. And although others have deemed my work innovative and transformational, what can I possibly say to anyone after witnessing so many Black women experience burnout and leave organizations and programs in droves? What words of hope could I possibly give to anyone after experiencing one of the darkest moments in my academic career? How and why should I put my pen to paper when the world continues to witness and ignore the anger for our fallen sisters and Black women have to keep explaining repeatedly our pain and reason for being (Lorde)?

Two years ago, when I considered leaving academia, a dear friend asked me a critical question that shook me to the core: "What does joy look like for an academic?" And while it wasn't the first time that someone had asked me a question about my professional academic desires or aspirations, it made me pause, because in my attempt to create counterspaces where others could find joy in science, I forgot to give myself the very same gift as an educator, mentor, multicultural navigator

(Carter), leader, and student. When did the work I love become such a burden? Was the source of my burnout a result of operating from a damage-centered frame? What kind of messages was I modeling for my students, who seemed to look up to me? Was I not deserving of joy too?

Recently, a dear mentor reminded me of the very same thing I always tell my mentees: "(Y)our story matters and will matter to someone. Tell your story." Well, let me forewarn you, I don't sing (at least professionally), and I don't have the voice or pen(wo)manship of Tracy Chapman to woo the masses. I do hope, though, that if you stay after reading about the lessons that I've learned, you will join me in my learning journey on how we can better orchestrate our furies so that they do not lead to the increased weathering of our racialized bodies and souls (Geronimus; Lorde). Or perhaps, you will find that any other place would be better, jump in a fast car, and leave the academy. Whatever you decide, I hope that someday you will reclaim your Joy of Missing Out (JOMO) and share your transformation story of hope or inspiration, because, as Lorde notes: "We use whatever strengths we have fought for, including anger, to help define and fashion a world where all our sisters can grow, where our children can love, and where the power of touching and meeting another woman's difference and wonder will eventually transcend the need for destruction" (133).

IMAGINING POSSIBILITIES

To be truly visionary we have to root our imagination in our concrete reality while simultaneously imagining possibilities beyond that reality.
—BELL HOOKS, *FEMINISM IS FOR EVERYBODY: PASSIONATE POLITICS*

About eight years ago, I was asked to work with a sixth grader on a science project. For this project, students were expected to pose a question, conduct an experiment, and present the findings on a poster board. When I asked this budding scientist if they had produced a research question, they enthusiastically replied, "Yes, I want to know which liquid grows a plant the fastest." In my mind, I thought, "Oh no! I don't know any biology. Could they not have chosen another topic, say in chemistry?" I then followed up and asked what made that particular topic so interesting. They paused and said, "Well, I'm curious to know if instead of water, could there be another liquid that could grow our plants? And if so, what liquid would that be?" I smiled and said, "I think a lot of people would be curious to know the same. So, let's design an experiment to see what we learn."

In the summer of 2020, when conversations about race were at the forefront of every institution's (re)commitment to equity and justice, Dr. Beronda Montgomery—scientist, scholar, administrator, and featured facilitator—put forward a critical reflection in a workshop whereby she offered a detailed analogy from previous work she had done between the cultivation and care of house plants and mentoring for students and faculty from diverse backgrounds. For instance, pointing out that since "we extensively probe our environment when the plants in it are not faring well," rather than immediately assuming a deficit in the plant, she posits that we should apply the same principle and translate our responses to plants to the care of students and colleagues—namely, we should begin with "asking systematic questions about the impact of the environment on an individual's potential for growth and success" ("From Deficits to Possibilities" 5). In short, she implores us to question how we can move from seeing deficits and failures to supporting and enabling possibilities.

I can still vividly remember the reactions from the attendees in our Zoom room when they heard this metaphor. It was as if, for the first time, everyone—scientists, engineers, graduate students, faculty, staff, and administrators—understood what it meant to be equity-minded. It was truly astonishing and, if I may be frank, scary to observe. Because for those of us whose racialized and gendered social interactions have often made us feel anxious, stressed, othered, and isolated, these questions provided a frame that validated our experiences and reminded us that the system was never built with us in mind. And just as with the sixth grader's research question about plant growth, Montgomery's perspective presents an opportunity and a call to action for us to reimagine what care work in higher education could look like.

Given the rise and effects of recent legislative backlash aimed at academic freedom and diversity efforts across higher education, the current state of affairs begets several questions for institutional leadership: How do we provide trauma-informed care and support for Black scholars' academic development and scholarship during trying times? How do we foster the next generation of Black academic leaders attuned to higher education's challenges? How do we proactively include appropriate expertise and practices to address conflict and disruptions (Montgomery and Whittaker)? I shall not attempt to say that I have all the answers. I, however, do posit that there remains a need for us to shift from a damage-centered frame to a desire-centered approach that "understands the complexity, contradiction, and the self-determination of lived lives" (Tuck 416). If we are truly committed to nurturing emerging Black women leaders, then we must consider the expansiveness of their existence (Toliver), so that they can thrive, experience unspeakable joy (Okello), and, most importantly, live.

Before I attempt to present any leadership development pathway for emerging Black women leaders, it is important that I share a bit about my journey into what I more broadly define as inclusive excellence work. This chapter will draw on critical lessons from my almost twenty years of collective learning experiences as a student, scientist, educational developer, and novice ethnographic researcher, working with students, faculty, staff, and academic leadership. I will then attempt to extend Montgomery's groundskeeping-centered leadership framework ("Academic Leadership") and propose a trauma-informed frame (Francis) to consider as I reconceptualize, develop, and operationalize academic leadership development for Black women that is justice-centered and responsive to seismic political shifts.

> *Make up a story for our sake and yours. Forget your name in the street; tell us what the world has been to you in the dark places and in the light. Don't tell us what to believe, what to fear. Show us belief's wide skirt and the stitch that unravels fear's caul.*
>
> —TONI MORRISON, *THE NOBEL LECTURE IN LITERATURE, 1993*

I will never forget that early spring afternoon when I received a notification that the article was officially live. This was the second time in two years that I had never seen a mockup before publication, so I was nervous. I will begin by saying that the journalist was a gracious interviewer, and they really made sure that I felt comfortable during the process and readily sought my input during their research. But people who know me will tell you that I have always been careful about the words I choose to convey messages related to my research or the people with whom I work. As for my students, they review and approve all communication before I share their accomplishments or work. And while I know they trust me, I do this to remind them that they are the captain of their ship, and they get to decide how they show up to the world.

I finally looked at the headline and gasped. The four words "inspiring university DEI efforts" immediately stood out to me. Oh, not DEI! I don't use that acronym in my work. But then I thought, is that all that people see in my work? Will I be pigeonholed or labeled as a "DEI" person? What will the leadership think? Do they even see my work as an institutional lift, as the title suggested? Most importantly, what about the other people who have been doing the work long before me? Would this title suggest their work wasn't as impactful? So many thoughts and questions filled my head. Why? Because I know the power of words and publicity.

Shortly after, I gathered myself and read the opening sentence: "*Dr. Tam'ra-Kay Francis was feeling a little nervous. The confession was a surprise given all she has accomplished*" (Stiffler). A calm came over me. She had perfectly captured how I felt when she told me that they wanted to shift the focus of the story to center my work, as my initiatives had been unique, impressive, and impactful. And while most people would be excited about being featured in one of the top national technology news sites in the country, I wasn't. While I appreciated the compliment and was grateful that others recognized my efforts, I always tell people I don't do this work for me. I also try to remind others that so many people are doing this work and have been doing this for years. My worry about being celebrated publicly is that I would once again be pulled away from my research to support other faculty in expanding their portfolios without receiving any citational credit or partnership, at least in a tangible way that the academy would value.

Then came a note from a senior administrator I had met a few months prior. They said they read the article, and it was a well-deserved recognition of everything I had been doing. Their thoughtfulness completely took me by surprise, not because of who they were, but because our first encounter remained imprinted on my mind. It wasn't too long before receiving the note that I had posed some questions to a second senior administrator and offered a recommendation that our council provide a space for their unit to share a bit about their work. The next thing I knew, I was caught up in an email chain with a third administrator, who happened to be the supervisor of the author of the kind note. So, you can imagine how worried I was that my initial emails echoing some frustration would be misinterpreted and my concerns dismissed. Thankfully, that wasn't the case, and everyone received the feedback well, so much so that they considered my recommendation, and happily agreed to speak to our group.

The meeting was amazing, and one of the best that I had attended all year. My colleagues were fully engaged and asked some really good questions. It made me happy because something in my heart told me that this would be of interest to others, and I was right. So, while others may argue that the note they sent to me was just a part of their job, I believed in my heart that their congratulatory words came from a sincere place, unlike those who still to this day haven't said anything or acknowledged my communication.

I know some of you must be thinking, why not live in the moment and smell the flowers? It has never been your thing to worry about the opinions of others, so why now? For those who understand gatekeeping, in the grand scheme of things I was just a postdoctoral appointee with no formal title, operating in a space that wasn't part of my assignment. I was never elected or groomed into an official role that fit the leadership profile of those typically featured on this new site. And yes, while I am aware that people get busy, I couldn't shake the feeling that this feature—though meant for good—may have inadvertently accelerated my pet-to-threat journey (Thomas et al., "Women of Color at Midcareer: Going from Pet to Threat"). So, for me, the feature could be read in one of two frames: (i) We are super proud of you, and we are happy others see it too, or (ii) Who do you think you are?

WHO DO YOU THINK YOU ARE?

I could argue that my first engagement with what we all now broadly describe as diversity, equity, and inclusion (DEI) was my work with an educational program in Philadelphia that aimed to provide rising sixth through tenth graders with educational resources, as well as my formal education at an HBCU. However, I believe my experiences with institutional equity-focused efforts began with the appointment of the inaugural vice chancellor of diversity and inclusion at the institution where I launched my doctoral journey. As a student, I wasn't sure what that all meant but I figured it must be good to have an institution strategically think about and publicly commit to advancing diversity. In my own workspace, our programs were already tailored to supporting students who were first-generation, low-income, and those with disabilities. So, when the call was made for our program to report to the new Office of Diversity and Inclusion, it seemed like a perfect fit.

Meanwhile, in my own nonwork graduate student sphere, a group of us had been meeting to create an organization that centered and supported racially minoritized graduate students. In our founding year, I was appointed to the role of Student Government Association Senator, which I now can say was the primer to my university governance learning journey. This role came at an interesting time for the university, as our chancellor and inaugural chief diversity officer (CDO) became the subjects of legislative attempts to dismantle diversity efforts. It was an interesting space for me to be in as a graduate student working with a program with a reporting line to our CDO. A year later, I would take on a role that would forever change the way I viewed academic leadership, student support, educational development, and equity.

In 2017, I developed the Universal Nexus for Inclusive Teaching Excellence (UNITE) six-point planning model to guide the Center for Teaching's educational development efforts with faculty and graduate students at the University of Tennessee. This framework was based on the theory of change that states that institutional cultural change is complex, and any efforts to advance inclusive excellence in the formal and informal curriculum would require strong synergistic partnerships between academic affairs, student affairs, and educational developers (Banks; Williams et al.; Nalty)—three areas that have supported me in my professional journey as a student, staff member, and instructional faculty member. At the micro and meso levels, my hypothesis was that, even without wholesale changes to an existing curriculum, program, or initiative, student-facing faculty and staff could use this model to reflect on and discuss where their individual strengths and opportunities for growth were moving toward being more inclusive from their sphere of influence.

After receiving feedback from faculty, graduate students, and administrators about the usefulness of the model, I slowly began adapting it for other programming, and this model would eventually become my very own change management framework. In fact, to date, every program that has been deemed innovative or successful was built from a curriculum that infused some variation of these six elements. How does the saying go? If it ain't broke, why fix it?

WHAT DOES UNSPEAKABLE JOY LOOK LIKE FOR YOU?

In the Fall of 2020, after completing an interdisciplinary tri-campus series titled Pedagogy and Research on Race, Identity, Social Justice, and Meaning (PR^{2}ISM), one of the biggest programs I have built to date, I began having difficulties swallowing and sleeping at night. It was one of the most frightening periods of my life because at times it felt as if my throat were closing in and I couldn't breathe. I did not go to the doctor right away because COVID-19 was a threat, we were deep in lockdown, and all the protocols for visits had changed. I also made three 911 calls, and, on the second visit, the paramedic team said I was fine and probably overly anxious. On the third call, they basically told me that unless I wasn't breathing, it wasn't an emergency. Since I couldn't get an appointment for a while, my family and friends would take turns staying up with me as I drank my chamomile tea to fall asleep. My fear? I would stop breathing.

One night, I called my cousin, a healthcare worker, in a panic because I didn't know what to do and needed someone on the phone in the event something happened. She then said to me, "I want you to BREATHE! Inhale for five seconds, hold for five seconds, and breathe out through your mouth for five seconds. I will count and we will do it together. Got it?" After several rounds of the exercise, she advised me to do these two or three times a day to help me gain control of my breathing. I was so intrigued I began to research focused breathing, because no one had ever told me about this.

I started doing this every night as I drank my tea until I got an appointment and more specific news about my health status. I finally learned that it wasn't anxiety and wasn't all in my head as the doctor had suggested when I went to urgent care two weeks into lockdown. I was sick and needed to prepare for major surgery in two weeks—during a raging pandemic. It was as if I was experiencing a delayed reaction to all the things I tried to shield my students and colleagues from. I was no longer invincible.

It has been both a quite rewarding and quite stressful journey engaging in change work over the past eight years as political efforts to curtail diversity-focused initiatives steadily increase. Building within and across units allowed me to learn more about institutional governance, which in turn gave me valuable tools to help others navigate oftentimes, sadly, unfortunate situations. And while having a seat at decision-making tables has been eye-opening to say the least, I really wish I had been much kinder to my younger self. I wish I had taken the time to slow down, reflect, and celebrate the way I encourage my mentees to do. Somewhere along the line, I kept the focus on the work, ignored my body, and almost lost my life and mind.

CREATING CULTURALLY AFFIRMING SPACES TO PREVENT BLACK DEATH

In essence, Black death precedes and is necessary for the enactment— often performatively—of institutional social justice efforts. Accordingly, policy and practice connected to diversity, equity, and inclusion, referred to as DEI, accurately reframed can be designated as DIE—a state in which the efforts of justice do not take place until the principal ingredient of Black death is added.

—DANIEL JOSIAH THOMAS III, MARCUS WAYNE JOHNSON & LANGSTON CLARK, "YOU'RE NOBODY UNTIL SOMEBODY KILLS YOU: THE INGREDIENTS OF BLACK DEATH FOR SOCIAL JUSTICE AND ~~DEI~~ DIE"

In the winter of 2023, the chemistry community lost two talented Black PhD students, whom I shall call Jennifer and Ryan, within two weeks of each other. To put the significance of their loss to the academic chemistry community in context, on average about two thousand doctoral degrees are awarded annually in chemistry and, of those, fifty are awarded to students who are racialized as Black. So, you can imagine how shaken the community was when they heard about their untimely passing. I remember both faculty and students reaching out to me to discuss support and resources for students.

I didn't know Ryan, but I knew Jennifer. We followed each other on social media and formally met after she reached out about a grant proposal that she was working on. Jennifer was an amazing leader and believed that networks are central to healing the community from racial traumas that prevent us from staying in STEM fields. Back in 2020, she and two other Black women chemists created an online nonprofit counterspace designed to amplify and support Black scientists in the chemical sciences across the world with opportunities and networks. Through this community, I have found financial and professional development opportunities for my students that I don't believe I otherwise would have had access to. I tell aspiring Black chemists that even at its core, the accessible space serves as a reminder that we are here and we are talented.

To support students as they processed the events after the death of George Floyd, in June of 2020 I created an online mobile mentoring program called "Dear Black Student." To help me get started, I reached out to thirty-five of my mentors, past students, and friends, and asked them to co-lead sessions on a variety of topics with me. They agreed without hesitation, and in three short days we launched the event. I also asked each of my guests to write letters so that any student who couldn't attend or anyone across the country could see their messages. Soon thereafter, several institutions reached out to me and asked if this opportunity was open to other spaces. I was flabbergasted. What I thought was the simplest gift we could give to students turned out to be what most of us needed at the time: a counterspace to grieve, breathe, and reclaim our joy.

At some point I might release these letters from the time machine vault, but for now, I'd like to leave you with some advice that saved my life: First and foremost, it is important to remember that you are not required to set yourself on fire to keep others warm. Your power is wielded in your ability to act and stand still. As much as you are able to, surround yourselves with people who will fight for you when you are not in the room. I am here because so many people stood in the gaps for me. It wasn't easy adopting a new mindset, but I had to choose myself, because in doing so, I get to model what healthy behaviors look like for young Black women.

The onset of the triple pandemic highlighted the contradiction between the current operating model of academic leadership and the goals of equity-seeking organizations. In response, we witnessed a proliferation of public statements and strategic plans from institutions committing their support to advancing diversity, equity, and inclusion (DEI), specifically, the recruitment and retention of Black scholars. At the same time, we saw two concurrent trends: an increased reliance on Black scholars to provide DEI-related guidance and the Great Resignation of Black scholars at all academic levels.

And if that weren't already concerning, we are now witnessing the cascading effects of the Supreme Court's 2023 ruling ending race-conscious affirmative action in college admission programs. In this current legislative session alone, over thirty states have introduced or passed more than one hundred anti-DEI bills aimed to regulate free speech, tenure, and public spending on diversity offices and programs in higher education (Adams and Chiwaya). To say these coordinated political and legal attacks are a surprise would be a half-truth. Having previously lived in the first state to successfully defund a diversity office at a public institution, I have witnessed firsthand how important it is for those doing this work to be proactive as we seek to build and sustain culturally affirming spaces in these times.

#DEARBLACKEMERGINGLEADERS: WHAT DOES THE MISSING OUT LOOK LIKE FOR YOU?

I tell my students, "When you get these jobs that you have been so brilliantly trained for, just remember that your real job is that if you are free, you need to free somebody else. If you have some power, then your job is to empower somebody else. This is not just a grab-bag candy game."
—TONI MORRISON, "THE TRUEST EYE"

A few months ago, I had an impromptu check-in with a professional mentor and coach. I was super excited to meet because I needed a sound voice that had no connections to my work. As I gave my updates, they paused softly and asked me how I was doing. I'd say I'm fairly good at keeping my composure in public spaces, but that day so much was weighing on my soul, and I broke down in tears. After handing me a napkin, they said, "TK, I could feel your anxiety and I knew something was wrong. Know that it is okay to cry here, but I also want you to BREATHE."

After I took a few breaths and dried my tears, I shared what was troubling me. As we continued talking, I shared the question my friend had asked about joy for my academic self. They looked at me and said, "I think that is a wonderful question because you're deserving of the same things you provide to everyone else, but I want to add another perspective. Have you heard about JOMO?" I paused and curiously replied, "No." They went on to explain that they believed that often one of the primary obstacles to finding our own joy is what people call the fear of missing out (FOMO). This is because we are so preoccupied with finding more activities to do, or what others think we should be doing, that we forget to be fully present and engaged. And if we're not careful in managing these fears, it can lead to us feeling even more stressed and anxious.

The Joy of Missing Out (JOMO) on the other hand, asks us to intentionally carve out time to disconnect without feeling guilty about missing out. My mentor, for example, shared that they, for example, have dedicated time each week to playing their favorite sport and sprucing up the garden—no phone calls, no social media, no emails. They then acknowledged that it must be hard for Black women in academia to "miss out" when showing up might give you the access you need to advance your career.

I've never been a fan of the latest craze, but I must admit I have been thinking a lot about JOMO and how that manifests in a heteronormative patriarchal society. What might this look like for those organizing, building, and supporting others? What might "missing out" on this look like for Black women in academia? How can organizations use the groundskeeping frame to enable possibilities for us to cultivate joy and genius simultaneously for Black women? More importantly, how can we utilize this framework to evaluate their commitments and keep ourselves accountable as a partner? In *We Want to Do More Than Survive*, activist and author Bettina Love reminds us: "Joy is crucial for social change; Joy is crucial for teaching. Finding joy during pain and trauma is the fight to be fully human. A revolutionary spirit that embraces joy, self care, and love is moving towards wholeness. Acknowledging joy is to make yourself aware of your humanity, creativity, self-determination, power, and ability to love abundantly" (119).

FROM GATEKEEPING TO GROUNDSKEEPING

In STEM, a gatekeeper or gateway course is one that students struggle to complete, preventing them from pursuing their intended major (Dai and Cromley). While the reasons may vary, a growing body of research suggests that a student's experience in introductory math and science classes is one of the primary barriers to their performance and success (Gasiewski et al.). It should come as no surprise then that these are the same courses that disproportionately push racially minoritized students out of these fields. As a result, the federal government and institutions have made significant investment in student support services, faculty and curricular development, and supplemental instruction to support both faculty and students to stop the "pipeline leakage."

But just like STEM educators have always acknowledged an increased need for intentional care work as we support our students, shouldn't institutions do the same when it comes to supporting Black women's leadership development? Because, frankly, until institutions understand the complexity and interrelatedness between human social systems and systemic racism (Banaji et al.) and how that contributes to the continued weathering on Black women's well-being and success, I do not see a sustainable leadership development pathway or pipeline for Black women in academia.

I read somewhere recently that this is the first time in history that we've had four generations working in the same workplace. That really stood out to me because I don't think the average academic leader thinks about their institutional cultural capital in ways that they should. Yes, I may have had the idea, but I couldn't have accomplished all that I have without the support of administrators who embraced expertise beyond hierarchies, structures, and titles. This is why Montgomery's concept of groundskeeping-centered leadership stood out to me:

> In this kind of progressive leadership leaders and mentors show others how to find their niche, how to assess the impact of the environment on growth and behavior, how to address and respond to competition, how to allocate energy to significant endeavors, and how to determine the effect of environmental history on community members. Rather than teaching tactical leadership skills to their successor, the wise leader

must cultivate leadership philosophies and vision. This kind of vision is needed to adapt to change in circumstances, and it can also enable leaders to see the potential collaborations and benefits in diverse communities. This approach contrasts with the traditional gatekeeping approach in which leaders determine who gains access via conceptualizations and assumptions about who can function and thrive in a particular context. (148–49)

The future of work will require a multidirectional and multigenerational leadership strategy that brings together expertise across the organization, including many who oftentimes sit at the margin, who can bring in the necessary skills needed for new growth and sustainability. Extending Montgomery's groundskeeping-centered leadership framework, I argue that it is incumbent on academic leadership purporting equity-centered efforts to examine the gatekeeping function of linear pathways to academic leadership for Black women and proactively protect and support them. Groundskeeping calls for a fundamental shift away from damage-centered and traditional gatekeeping practices and brings Black women's cultural capital and expertise to the forefront of their educational development experience. In this holistic framework, intentional care work is made to deconstruct the hidden curriculum and provide full access to the resources and tools needed to cultivate Black women's identity development, intellect, and creative engagement.

As I reflected on my experiences in higher education and considered how I might contribute to a conversation about academic Black women leaders, I wrestled with several things. The first is that there already exists a wealth of research studies on leader development. How then would I ensure that this chapter extends that body of work in ways that would be meaningful to Black women in predominantly white spaces? And if I do this, whose voices should I be centering? The second was my experience as an academic leader. Although a quick scan of my CV would reveal that I have successfully designed and implemented several institution-wide projects at two large research universities, you will find that none of these roles were linked to a salaried administrator position. This would therefore mean that my insights would be limited to experiences of working administrators, and the testimonials and lessons from my mentors. Last but certainly not least is something I wish my younger self had tapped into years ago: a critical examination of Black life in America. While I draw on the wisdom of Black scholars, particularly those engaged in Black critical feminist work, this is a relatively new interdisciplinary learning journey for me. As a trained chemist, now a STEM educator, I cannot overstate the importance of the work of my colleagues in the humanities and the social sciences in providing the necessary nutrients for me to grow in this work.

One of the things I've learned during my time as a university graduate student leader is that most people do not have a clear understanding of their institution's identity and its governance structure. The irony is that although this kind of informational capital is often publicly available, it is not readily shared or discussed unless you are in a leadership position.

Because this groundskeeping framework requires a desire-centered approach to building members' cultural capital, the application and operationalization of each dimension will look different across institution types and governance structures.

Institutional leaders committed to cultivating a pipeline of groundskeeping leaders will have to perform routine assessments to create interventions that are responsive to their constituents' needs. This type of caretaking leadership requires leaders to step away from the traditional ivory tower approach and essentially become critical researchers. At the core of the transformation is the idea that if everyone did their part to be intentional about infusing evidence-based inclusive strategies in their respective learning spaces, they would become catalysts who generate a transformational shift in Black women's learning outcomes, persistence, and overall sense of belonging.

Earlier I shared some of my collective experiences and insights through what I now call the six dimensions of groundskeeping. While this framework can be used by institutions to develop interventions, we have a shared responsibility in this partnership. This means that the onus will be on us to conduct our own culturally responsive evaluation of the working and learning environments we choose to call our academic home, making these critical next step decisions for a healthy you.

WORKS CITED

Adams, Char, and Nigel Chiwaya. "Map: See Which States Have Introduced or Passed Anti-DEI Bills." *NBC News*, Mar. 2 2024, https://www.nbcnews.com/data-graphics/anti-dei-bills-states-republican-lawmakers-map-rcna140756.

Banaji, Mahzarin R., et al. "Systemic Racism: Individuals and Interactions, Institutions and Society." *Cognitive Research*, vol. 6, no. 82, 2021. *Springer Open*, https://doi.org/10.1186/s41235-021-00349-3.

Banks, James A., and Cherry A. McGee Banks. *Multicultural Education: Issues and Perspectives.* 10th ed., Wiley, 2019.

Carter, Prudence L. *Keepin' It Real: School Success Beyond Black and White.* Oxford UP, 2007.

Chapman, Tracy. "Fast Car." Elektra Records, New York, 1988.

Dai, Ting, and Jennifer G. Cromley. "Changes in Implicit Theories of Ability in Biology and Dropout from STEM Majors: A Latent Growth Curve Approach." *Contemporary Educational Psychology*, vol. 39, no. 3, 2014, pp. 233–47. *Science Direct*, https://doi.org/10.1016/j.cedpsych.2014.06.003.

Francis, Tam'ra-Kay Alisia. *Exploring Professional Teaching Identity Development for STEM Graduate Teaching Assistants (GTAs).* 2018. University of Tennessee, Knoxville, PhD dissertation.

Gasiewski, Josephine A., et al. "From Gatekeeping to Engagement: A Multicontextual, Mixed Method Study of Student Academic Engagement in Introductory STEM Courses." *Research in Higher Education*, vol. 53, no. 2, Mar. 2012, pp. 229–61. *Springer Nature*, https://doi.org/10.1007/s11162-011-9247-y.

Geronimus, Arline. "The Weathering Hypothesis and the Health of African American Women and Infants: Evidence and Speculations." *Ethnicity and Disease*, vol. 2, no. 3, summer 1992, pp. 207–21.

Lorde, Audre. "The Uses of Anger: Women Responding to Racism." *Sister Outsider: Essays and Speeches*. The Crossing Press, 1984.

Love, Bettina L. *We Want to Do More Than Survive: Abolitionist Teaching and the Pursuit of Educational Freedom*. Beacon Press, 2019.

Montgomery, Beronda L. "Academic Leadership: Gatekeeping or Grounds-keeping?" *The Journal of Values-Based Leadership*, vol. 13, no. 2, 2020. *Valpo-Scholar*, https://doi.org/10.22543/0733.132.1316.

———. "From Deficits to Possibilities: Mentoring Lessons from Plants on Cultivating Individual Growth Through Environmental Assessment and Optimization." *Public Philosophy Journal*, vol. 1, no. 1, spring 2018. *Kora*, https://projects.kora.matrix.msu.edu/files/6-15-173284/Montgomery Beronda.FromDeficitstoPossibilitiesPPJ1.1Spring2018.pdf.

Montgomery, Beronda L., and Joseph A. Whittaker. "The Roots of Change: Cultivating Equity and Change Across Generations from Healthy Roots." *The Plant Cell*, vol. 34, no. 7, July 2022. *PubMed*, https://doi.org/10.1093/plcell/koac121.

Nalty, Kathleen B. *Going 'All-In' on Diversity and Inclusion: The Law Firm Leader's Playbook*. PBC, 2015.

Okello, W. K. "Unspeakable Joy: Anti-Black Constraint, Loopholes of Retreat, and the Practice of Black Joy." *Urban Education*, 31 Jan. 2024. *Sage Journals*, https://doi.org/10.1177/00420859241227956.

Stiffler, Lisa. "'Incredible Impact': This Researcher Is Bolstering STEM Students and Inspiring University DEI Efforts." *Geekwire*, May 2022, https://www.geekwire.com/2022incredible-impact-this-incredible-impact-this-researcher-is-bolstering-stem-students-and-inspiring-university-dei-efforts.

Thomas, Kecia M., et al. "Women of Color at Midcareer: Going from Pet to

Threat." *Psychological Health of Women of Color: Intersections, Challenges, and Opportunities*, edited by Lillian Comas-Díaz and Beverly Greene. Praeger, 2013, pp. 275–86.

Toliver, Stephanie R. "Just, At Least, Try to Understand. Culturally Situated Reader Response and Curriculum Curation for Black Girls." *Journal of Curriculum and Pedagogy*, 8 Feb. 2024, pp. 1–26, https://doi.org/10.1080/15505170.2024.2312111.

Tuck, Eve. "Suspending Damage: A Letter to Communities." *Harvard Educational Review*, vol. 79, no. 3, 2009, pp. 409–28.

Williams, Damon A., et al. *Toward a Model of Inclusive Excellence and Change in Postsecondary Institutions*. Association of American Colleges and Universities, 2005, https://operations.du.edu/sites/default/files/2020-04/model-of-inclusive-excellence.pdf.

5

INTERCULTURAL DIMENSIONS AND HIGHER EDUCATION LEADERSHIP

Barriers and Stepping Stones for Black Women Professionals in Unique Predominantly White Institutions

JANICE D. M. MITCHELL

Being a Black woman who has the audacity to aspire to leadership, we're always going to be judged by a different set of standards.
—MAYOR LORI LIGHTFOOT, QTD. IN APRIL RYAN,
Black Women Will Save the World: An Anthem

As we consider the disparity of Black women professors' leadership in academe, we may well have forgotten about the role cultural dimensions play in achieving leadership positions in predominantly white institutions (PWIs). Teaching and leading on the defense require tackling hurdles that are often determined by cultural *mindsets* and *perceptions* (Harushimana et al.). Three such *mindsets* can be:

- Mindset 1: Overall Competency Mindsets (Linguistic/ Communication and Leadership)

- Mindset 2: The Level of Respect for the Need for Diversity and Inclusion through Equity in Higher Education
- Mindset 3: Competence and Allyship Meet Age in the Academy of Leadership

Mindsets are worldviews. Mindsets lead to assumptions. Those assumptions can be strictly exported to the individual seeking academic recognition. Black faculty and administrators are always running a defense to stay ahead of the sometimes-offensive fallout based on culturally determined mindsets. Overshadowing obvious competence and leaning on other cultural determinants, mindsets, and assumptions, such as regard for race, gender, and age, can lead to competence invisibility.

MINDSET 1: OVERALL COMPETENCY MINDSETS

In addition to the intersectionality of race, gender, personality traits, language use, age, amount and type of experience, and educational level, professional jealousy can cast an unfortunate subjective shadow from others when one is trying to navigate the glass cliff in higher education. Realizing that all of these extras are predetermined by the time we arrive at the bottom of that glass cliff, Black women faculty moving on to administrative roles must be vigilant as they seek to move to each ledge of that cliff (Mthethwa-Sommers).

The cultural environment of our PWI campuses and institutions may require more of us than of others, or worse, expect less; in-house Black candidates just have to be careful that the assumptions made by the institution do not lead to *competence invisibility* when they envision a potential sustainable future there. At Gallaudet University, faculty, staff, and administrators are evaluated on several factors: their ability to communicate with students at different levels of hearing status and on their proficiency in using a language that is not their first language, namely

American Sign Language. This creates another ledge of the glass cliff to navigate and may be tied to all those other determinants and dimensions supporting or hindering one's growth as a faculty member or in leadership roles.

Black faculty must grapple with such issues in various types of institutions of higher learning. As our colleagues begin to look outside the classroom toward administrative roles, somehow leadership has boundaries that remain unspoken, as Black women in higher education begin to try to cross them. Those boundaries go back to intercultural dimensions tied to power (Hofstede), yet are also subjectively connected to the colleagues making the leadership selections and the level of objective belief as to who has the competence and skill to lead them. Add in linguistic competence as a skill variable and, in some instances, a definite political entity, and certain barriers may become even more evident.

MINDSET 2: RESPECT FOR THE NEED FOR DIVERSITY AND INCLUSION THROUGH EQUITY IN HIGHER EDUCATION

Respect for the values and tenets of a real commitment to diversity and inclusion initiatives must be in place throughout the campus landscape, but not without committing to how equity is visibly at work before equality can be realized completely. There is little room for the "Aren't we there yet?" attitude, as if on a road trip taking way too long to reach its destination.

I remember when the concept of political correctness (PC) came into our vocabulary. What Black professionals may have thought might wake up colleagues and the administration to the need for intercultural sensitivity as a tool toward equity became another umbrella under which to shield the distasteful idea that, on campuses of higher education, such values weren't already considered as understood. The joke was on me because I was already transcending that thinking in that I believed instead in being "humanly correct," or *HC*.

MINDSET 3: COMPETENCE AND ALLYSHIP MEET AGE IN THE ACADEMY OF LEADERSHIP

Competence invisibility is real in impeding the movement of Black leadership in higher education at PWIs. Ageism is real as well when it comes to a generational mindset of assumptions of just how much those Black academic leaders who have been very successful at various stages of their profession somehow outgrow their ability or willingness to mentor younger aspiring colleagues. It is important to know where that mindset may come from if present; mentors can also be allies, and vice versa. Sharing our own privilege of well-earned place and status is essential, but talented younger peers must also reach out to create such *an allyship* (Mitchell, "Who's Willing to Walk").

In her article, "Through a Glass, Darkly: The Hidden Injury of Ageism in the Academy," Peggy Johnson puts forth a writing format idea that combines lyrical essay, autoethnography, and sensemaking (Weick). These terms spoke to me as the writer of this piece, because we are in an era where a treatise of one's career and/or life's journey as a Black woman professor in a PWI with yet an additional special campus demographic, that is, the Deaf community, adds yet another ledge on the way up the glass cliff. Her work takes on a narrative character (often not thought to be scholarly) when, in fact, it is a critical, more literary introduction to the uniqueness of such a journey, connecting the dots of effective and often intense laboring toward a positive end (Reed-Danahay).

In Johnson's manner of defining a newer path of inquiry with the use of the format of the lyrical essay and autoethnography, she arrives at "blend[ing] memoir, research, and essay in a way that emphasizes the sharing of deeply felt emotions over and above the verifiable accuracy of information"

(Johnson 66). Not only does this shed light on how she perceived and processed her experiences, but also on how she navigated those experiences. She chose not to offer set conclusions but instead to highlight the interlocking web of circumstances and tried to make sense of how she had processed them (66).

MINDSET 1: OVERALL COMPETENCY MINDSETS

In my opening statement on competency mindsets, I highlighted that Black faculty must grapple with myriad intersectional issues in diverse types of institutions of higher learning. They must stay mindful of the unspoken hierarchical and sometimes personal boundaries when they try to cross them. After all, academe is a foundation built upon hierarchical leverage based upon a set of criteria. The nature of those criteria sets the stage for interpretation by the hierarchical framework itself and how an institution's faculty and staff set forth to structure that framework. This often may promote professional growth within the institution of those who wish at some point to be promoted within their departments or to other levels of administrative leadership and responsibility. Those boundaries are tied to the cultural dimension of power distancing (Hofstede).

Critical Incidents can be used as an ethnographic research tool to determine mindsets and attitudes. Brislin and Yoshida (1994) and Cushner and Brislin (1995) collaborated to give us useful training tools to help trainers prepare educators and others in how to successfully traverse a different cultural space either abroad or at home. The use of Critical Incidents has been especially useful in highlighting the positive and negative fallout faced when confronted with differently-abled others.

Mindset biases around hearing status and linguistic competence may play an important role here when the promotional transition is bound by one set of linguistic competence rules for an in-group faculty versus an out-group faculty, who had to learn the language in question within a six- to eight-week orientation program and were annually evaluated by everyone as to competence—peers, students, middle management, and other administrators, not all of whom were native users of the target language, in this case, American Sign Language (ASL). ASL is used by second language users who are hearing, not native users themselves. In addition, unlike language educators, evaluators may often not be trained in evaluating language competencies and skill sets. This is considered an important feature of these evaluations by language professionals. For example, in my personal forty-five-year experience such evaluations were also done each semester by classroom students who themselves do not use a fully standardized ASL, since they come from different parts of the country with varying backgrounds in English and ASL. Many are not aware that there is also the linguistic distinction of Black Signs within the language classifications of ASL. Imagine the type of biased commenting that may possibly come from those who find such dialectal/social vernacular or home language use difficult to understand! This would ultimately hold true in reverse, depending upon the amount of exposure young Black deaf students have had to their white counterparts, which also may be limited socially, but rarely educationally. The Black deaf student must do what is known to sociolinguistic researchers as code-switch. Ironically, white deaf peers may have to do the same thing with people from different geographic regions, bringing some interactional discomfort.

Only in recent years, as I neared retirement, did faculty decide to have incoming students be introduced to what would be considered as academic ASL, since the curriculum overhaul included mandatory student presentational work as a part of their class and end grade evaluations (Mitchell and McCaskill). For foreign language professionals using our *National Standards of Foreign Language Education* (American Council on the Teaching of Foreign Languages), presentational levels of communication are key. In other words, even our deaf colleagues realized that all of the various home signs brought to campus from across the nation as well as by international students from several countries needed some standardization by those who set the stage for linguistic research and development of ASL as a dynamic rather than static language in its own right. Success now would be determined by the use of integrational rubrics created by deaf and hearing academic faculty, developed by those certified in ASL use, and, in my case, also by student peers attending the mandatory class presentations and evaluating them by those same rubrics. I am not certain that other professors did their grading in this way; however, even with my forty-five years of experience using ASL as a classroom communication tool and generally in daily personal use, as a non-native user, and as a Black professor—a fairly new experience to most white students and international students of color—I felt it necessary to have deaf people who use ASL watch and evaluate the peer presenter according to more delineated and accepted norms as offered by our well-detailed rubrics.

As a linguist and consultant on intercultural competence across educational borders, admittedly, I had a unique perspective on linguistic competence, since I was teaching German using English and ASL both as means to communicate about and in the languages in the classroom and also abroad in Germany. The looks of disbelief that most students had when they realized that they were being taught German by a Black professor was something I decided to capitalize upon as a way to set the stage for the years of teaching my classes. After all, if they set aside their whiteness mindset and focused mainly on what made them white and different, that is, deafness, some began to identify with how difference can become an asset rather than a liability. For some of them, I became that role model. For a few, there were moments where they just withdrew for assorted reasons. Yet, Black deaf students would ask me if I liked music. When I said that I did very much and that I sang and loved dancing, too, they would smile and say, "I thought so!" Why? Because my language rhythm in ASL use had a rather musical flow to it; they responded, "Not a bad thing at all, just different."

Cadence in language use became a variable I had not factored into how I might be evaluated differently in the area of ASL classroom communication to the predominantly culturally-other students I taught weekly. Now it was not just about my profile of "hearing-ness," but also about personal body language added to the requirements of ASL protocols—both a professional and culturally personal area mixed into my career-determining aspirations, some of which could be altered, and some not. Here is the intersection where culturally-different other meets culturally-different other and now a cross-cultural interaction takes place that can be positive or negative, but, for certain, is interculturally sensitive both in exchange, information reception, and cross-cultural worldviews. Intercultural competence expertise after years of such encounters can go a long way toward bridging earlier tricky gaps in student comprehension of the discipline, other culture acceptance, and, ultimately, promotional evaluations by those you are teaching.

After many years of corrective measures to various testing instruments used to measure just how well hearing faculty were able to communicate in the classroom, it was evident that some of those measures themselves began with built-in flaws, as they were developed by the users themselves without any input from language professionals trained in how to put such testing measures into practice. Enter the Black professional language educator, the likes of whom many of those students, regardless of demographic, had never seen nor had as teachers. Add on the linguistic barriers created until such time as the faculty feel confident in communicating in ASL as they continue being trained and evaluated repeatedly (all before ever being considered for tenure), and the stage is set for tenacious determination to either stay the course or to pull up stakes and move on with partial skill in a rather societally romanticized language experience. When you do stay, it is because you realize ASL is the lifeblood running through the veins of the Deaf community and its culture and it becomes a matter of your career survival. All this is in addition to your competence in your specific discipline, and because you have decided you wish to stay for a variety of reasons.

CRITICAL INCIDENTS: EVALUATION FOR PROMOTION AND MERIT RAISE

As mentioned before, in my institution a particularly important evaluative tool installed is that of ongoing testing of sign language competence. It is explained upon hiring that such testing will be ongoing until an established level is reached, required within three years without interpreter assistance and determined by a person or designated team of ASL users. Most faculty being evaluated this way think that it is mainly about classroom competence. However, the longer you stay in the community, the easier it becomes to expect more competence in all aspects of ASL use that fit Deaf culture. This may mean a quite different expectation of competence if faculty have not considered, versus are considering becoming fully integrated into the Deaf community and thereby in its culture on a daily basis, and often beyond regular university duties. That feature may well determine one's longevity as faculty. The situation is similar to that of an individual studying abroad, living with a host family, and participating in a summer program where one must learn not only the language of the country but also the culture of the people and their histories.

On a particular occasion while preparing my merit increase portfolio that also included a promotion, I took the evaluation test as required. I waited and waited for my results, which would ultimately result in whether or not I got the promotion. As this was a time-sensitive issue, of course I became concerned, not yet having received my results. I requested a meeting with the testing staff. What ensued revealed results that seemed to be inequitable and discriminatory.

During the explanation given to me while I watched a replay of my video testing, I felt that my evaluation results had been skewed. I sat wondering what the problem was until the tester/evaluator put Post-it notes on the monitor to cover my face, leaving only my hands to be watched. It might appear to be acceptable and fair if sign language were only about the hands. However, facial expression along with hands and body language is a linguistic feature to be considered as a part of how well one communicates when signing. That important part of my video was hidden during the results explanation that suggested I had just missed passing the level required. I challenged this outcome primarily because one whole piece of the communication process in ASL is expressive facial expressions (for example, eyebrow movement and eye contact). The observation by the student that my signing had a more rhythmic communicative style that did not impair comprehension when I signed was an added linguistic feature that, as a Black hearing signer, would give a different cadence to my signing. My signing when speaking was a different rhythm than signing when not using my voice, another preferred feature of ASL that also played a role. That this feature had been removed completely was the first challenge.

The second challenge to the results had to do with one sign used in particular, that is, the sign for "German/Germany" is one sign for both the language and the country. You might ask, what difference does that make? There is a great deal of difference in how one teaches a spoken language with a written grammar versus using a non-oral language where there is no distinction between a country and the language, as discussed in my dissertation, *The Relationship of Foreign Language Training to the Written Grammar and Written English of Deaf College Students and the Implications for Teaching the Written Grammars of Spoken Languages to the Postsecondary Hearing Impaired.* In my effort to make clear and very visible to my students that they were not the same word when writing and translating from sign to English or German, I actually attached (with their knowledge) a "-y" at the end of my sign for "German," which hit home with them and was permissible suffix usage at that time in the progression of sign language usage on campus, that is, to add on suffixes, such as verb endings "-s/-es," "-ed," "-ing." This was done during that stage of ASL development to ensure clarity of writing in English for all deaf students and speaking clarity for those hard of hearing or Cochlear

Implant deaf students. Subject matter learning often required additional aids to visible language reception.

I sat with a non-faculty tester who was a known Deaf community leader to explain this difference and why deaf students, in order to use another language fully and correctly, would need to actually *see* that language, using signing, *as it is written*, since there was only one sign that stood for both the language and the country. He was completely surprised at the need for that feature (perhaps not having been in a German elementary foreign language class) and agreed it surely made sense when teaching German to the students to make such a major distinction. He also agreed it in no way destroyed ASL comprehension and changed his assessment of my video performance. I did pass as required. I did get the merit increase and the promotion. I also realized that my classroom language signing might have to be altered when not in the classroom but also among deaf people in non-academic interactions, that is, a form of code-switching that is a familiar linguistic feature of how Black speech may change in vocabulary and rhythm when among friends and family or not. It can be a feature of choice in intercultural communication.

CRITICAL INCIDENT: PROFESSIONAL ADVANCEMENT

Over the years there were many other incidents that were overcome as obstacles to my professional movement as well as to my educational and intellectual integrity. Here I offer one example of a competence invisibility factor as I finally acceded to and served for three years as department chairperson after many years of teaching at all levels and scheduling, advising, mentoring, designing curriculum development, and fostering study abroad and a foreign language double major or minor in the secondary curriculum of the Teacher Certification Program, School of Education. As the glass cliff ledges were climbed onto along with university service in myriad ways over four decades, it was finally deemed that

I had indeed earned selection for chair after so long being overlooked and undervalued, especially in the areas of campus networking in advocacy that I brought to the position.

The outcomes of these three years before the aggressive move of my unseating were that: 1) much was achieved for both our students and my faculty, and 2) department stature was elevated from a position where it previously faced the threat of budget cuts. But the competence invisibility factor was made clear when the many accomplishments not heretofore made possible by previous chairpersonships were treated with little thanks or recognition. Part of that scenario, I came to understand, had its roots in the reality that the accomplishments could not have been fully realized without the dean's support, which the previous chair did not have. However, because I was able to garner the dean's respect for my ideas and suggestions, unlike the previous chair of nine years, some of the department faculty decided that these accomplishments could not have been the result of my ability to successfully cross administrative lines, no matter the number of rewards they received because of my competence, despite three turbulent years of protest-fallout that affected our budgets and general campus morale.

MINDSET 2: RESPECT FOR THE NEED FOR DIVERSITY AND INCLUSION THROUGH EQUITY IN HIGHER EDUCATION

It is necessary in discussions of diversity and inclusion through equity for institutions to start out on the same page in defining what those terms mean in reality. Just as difference brings diverse ideas to any discussion, that difference plays out in how each faculty member as a citizen defines them, that is, what they bring to campus with them. In addition, there is the distinction that can be made between needs and ideals, actively doing the right thing (however that is defined) versus talking about it, that is, advocacy, and embracing what those concepts mean versus tolerating what they espouse (Winters).

Earlier in the chapter, I suggested a coined concept of mine that I discussed at the 2009 Multicultural Education conference on campus: *humanly correct (HC)*. It came about when I realized that PC was now being used to initialize "politically correct" and not "people of color"— POC. And, since I was never a fan of using acronyms, nicknames, or labeling, it was disquieting to face the fact that we had yet another category in which to fit or, better said, into which to be placed by others. I chose, instead, to speak of being *humanly* or *humanely correct*. It is my suspicion that such an idea could lead us to finally arrive at our ultimate destination of fully embracing diversity and inclusion on our campus.

In one of my unpublished papers, I cover the idea of the multicultural divide being more of a border to be crossed than a dangerous moat to swim across in hopes of arriving unscathed at the other side. When Gallaudet University began to embark on tackling and laboring over diversity initiatives, I was right there. There were only a few Black voices that were being heard at the time, and I was determined one of them would be mine, as mine was the Black voice with the longest campus tenure at that time. However, other members of our Black faculty bring their own style of micro/macro-aggressive behaviors to the committee tables with them, and those can also stoke competence invisibility, or a shifting of the mindsets in the room about which Black voice is preferred over another. This is where the tenets of intercultural competence come into play, since it is actually cross-cultural interaction taking place at campus tables of exchange. For intercultural communication to happen, everyone at the table need not hold the same worldviews, but there must be an openness to diverse ways to perceive the same tasks and how to accomplish them (Mitchell and Murti, *Fostering and Promoting Inclusion*). Thus, I chose to be a leading voice on my campus for diversity initiatives.

In some writings and studies, I categorize *worldview* and *prejudice* as attitudes (Samovar and Porter; Mitchell, *The Relationship of Foreign*

Language Training). They are terms that describe how we see the world around us, which is shaped by our nuclear and extended families, our educational mentors and advisors, our classroom teachers, and of course, our friends. We may forget that faculty colleagues are also those people; and when they show up as department members in departmental meetings, committee faculty at faculty meetings, or institutional administrators comprising non-faculty staff, one's interaction with them still carries with it worldviews and prejudices. Those attitudes can both peripherally and significantly have an impact upon the goals and aspirations a Black professional woman professor/administrator may seek when establishing a solid career at the institution. This is where diversity, equity, and fairness intersect and added experience perhaps offers a new direction toward initiatives that foster inclusion.

In the introduction of Mindset 2, I mentioned the road trip analogy of "Aren't we there yet?" translated into "Can't we move on?" Respect for the values and tenets of a real commitment to diversity and inclusion initiatives must be in place throughout the campus landscape, but not without committing to how equity is visibly at work before equality can be realized completely. If that cannot be an honest and open commitment by which campus constituents and stakeholders interact, including board members, with this approach as their standard mission and vision, then being HC can stall, and intercultural insensitivity wins out.

CRITICAL INCIDENT: APPLYING AND INTERVIEWING FOR THE ASSOCIATE DEAN POSITION

The reorganization of our College of Arts and Sciences led to the new administrative restructuring, including a new position of associate dean. Heretofore, no such position was available, and eventually was available only to those selected as a Faculty Fellow, a kind of internal internship for which one could not apply but would instead be appointed in a role of assistance in the dean's offices. Openings of leadership did not often present themselves for Black faculty, where there were very few opportunities for moving into administration other than perhaps chairperson, occupied almost exclusively by white faculty, where one could be voted in again every three years or called to serve during sabbaticals or illness. In addition, the hearing versus deaf spoken and unspoken characteristics (the unspoken elephant in the room) also might historically play into who was really being considered from among the applicants.

Yet, after thirty-three years in an all-white department, a predominantly white administration, and being once mistaken for one of the secretaries who, at the time, were often Black women, I discussed with my family what a transition to associate dean might mean for me. After thirty-three years of making my own way to lead on committees in the Faculty Senate and University Council and serving as chairperson for the previous separate German department some years before, but still waiting for a turn at chairperson of this merged department, I applied for associate dean and felt well-prepared to fulfill all aspects of the positions, but two of those interviews yielded Critical Incidents.

In the first interview, a department head asked me why after thirty-three years I had just now applied for an administrative position. I answered truthfully and frankly, asserting that there were very few opportunities on campus for transitioning into administrative leadership positions, since they were often held so long by the same person(s); the barriers to faculty of color on campus moving into the few positions available was a fact easily documented, given the data of who's who on campus and where they resided; and that the false assumption had been made that I had no leadership experience in all that time. I had had a substantial leadership role in every campus diversity initiative along with having attained my Cultural Diversity Professional Certification (CDP) while doing so. I pointed out that my leadership skill building also came from other highly important visible executive directorships and chairpersonships off-campus and internationally.

The second interview was with the dean, who was a hard of hearing cultural gatekeeper herself. She asked a few questions after hearing my presentation, ending with "and how do you feel you manage stress?" I have to admit I did not expect that, but I answered the way most Black professional women with families and careers might. I felt rather good about the outcome of the interview despite the micro-aggressive inquiries.

Results came in. Another white woman faculty with whom most of us were not familiar before this process had been selected instead. In my mind I questioned whether the intersection of race and/or hearing played a role in this process. I decided to ask why I had not been selected. The answer, to my surprise, was that my presentation "sounded more like a dean's presentation than an associate's." I was stunned and speechless. I wondered how it could be that they would not want someone who could see the larger picture showing a vision that could only serve to support your challenges and programs as the dean and in the age of diversity, equity, and inclusion. I realized then that my main accomplishment had ultimately been full campus exposure and that I had the administrative wherewithal to do her job by the dean's own admission. Here again, though having worked together in past endeavors, the dean was indeed surprised herself; she had also succumbed to competence invisibility tinged with perhaps other factors. The laborer and cultural outsider must have brought clarity to how campus diversity and inclusion can work with the goal of equality through equitable opportunity in a meaningful and useful framework (Griffith).

MINDSET 3: COMPETENCE AND ALLYSHIP MEET AGE IN THE ACADEMY OF LEADERSHIP

Given the title of this book, the Johnson article title "Through a Glass, Darkly: The Hidden Injury of Ageism in the Academy" might have been one of the things that drew me to the article; I was attracted to the idea of how easily most glass can be broken, and the author's discussion of the hidden injury with relationship to age that can go unnoticed and often unattended among our ranks as Black professionals. In focusing on gender plus age and ranking, Johnson's use of laborers provides a highly relevant description transferable to those who labor in academe as they strive to become a part of institutions where they are definitely in the heritage minority, but bring with them their credentials and personal experiences. They can find themselves laboring daily not only to do a stellar job in the classroom, but also to determine the right timeline and timeframe to delve into the workings of the faculty committee structure and, perhaps over time, its institutional power hierarchy. Johnson also suggests that many institutions take a position that is at odds with those more experienced women faculty who experience marginalization and are made to feel invisible. They proceed as if the acts of injustice don't exist at their university and so may use the hiring of younger women at mid-level or lower-status positions as evidence that they are not gender-biased at all and are staying true to the diversity initiatives for hiring equitably (Acker; Gullette).

An example of unfounded obstacles to the promotion of Black women faculty might be borne out in the case of a Black deaf PhD in pursuit of first, achieving tenure, and later, the rank of full professor. Although she was well-known to the college community, I had met this faculty member as a student many years earlier. As she grew and matured in her career, the university structure was also in flux and had seen two community-altering boycotts around issues of deafness, access, visibility, and empowerment. In her effort to cement her continued career as a member of a department run by two white men on the faculty—one deaf and one hearing—she was repeatedly required to fulfill additional requirements that were unwarranted and were not a part of any of the guidelines set for faculty pursuing tenure or promotion. I learned of this firsthand when asked to write support letters for these additional requirements, since I was tenured and a full professor myself and a willing mentor. In each case, there were discrepancies surrounding her interviews and the acceptance of her career portfolios, which also included her research projects in Black Deaf Studies as well as her scholarly publications. By this time, I had been tenured for many years and asked to represent faculty to the Board as Vice Chair of the Faculty working on our bylaws and guidelines.

When she approached me in anguish about additional requirements expected of her beyond those required of any white women on the faculty and not warranted by our very clear guidelines, I directed her to our Faculty Guidelines and suggested that they be given as a refresher to those white men department heads, as they themselves had not achieved much of what she had already accomplished and none of the add-ons that they figured she would have little time to accomplish in order to meet the deadline for applying for her promotion. As we discuss the glass cliff we climb as Black women faculty in PWIs, such ledges are made steeper by those who find our ascension threatening to their own sense of worth in the institution. Ultimately, this example of career-stalking sometimes happens across race and gender and ages. The invisibility of competent talent wearing a different skin and clothing can be overcome only when there is someone experienced on those same ledges who is caring and staying vigilant. At this juncture, the generational aspects of competence came into play and gave support to the diligence and respect for the work and effort of a younger colleague. We crossed the generational divide, and the former student-professor relationship of previous years became one of respected colleagues co-teaching a very diverse-hearing group of students across the curriculum in Black Deaf Studies and Intercultural Competence. Such an example might fit under Johnson's section entitled, "The Institutional Response to Inequality" (69). At this stage, the glass cliff was at the department administrative level. The remedy was finding an ally, standing on principle, and demanding acknowledgment of superior achievement and earned respect using the same policies of equitable merit for all other such administrative procedures of advancement. Here older, more experienced allyship was essential in supporting the further climb by a younger colleague. I began this chapter by suggesting that there are various possible *mindsets* that play a role in how Black women professional academics are received on PWI campuses and welcomed into the hierarchical structures of the institutions we choose to join. The mindsets that either enhance our choices or hinder them are offered here in conclusion.

Ryan Gottfredson gives some key findings of his research on mindset differences across a few societal dimensions by ethnicity. The research shows how ethnicity can play a significant role in how groups respond to their environments and ultimately to those with whom they interact. The implications presented across Asian, Black/African American, Hispanic, and white/Caucasian groups suggests that the areas of difference with the most rigidity to change and acknowledgment of cultural differences rests within the white/Caucasian groups. This may be borne out by our experiences as Black people and, particularly, as Black women professionals in higher education. This is also exhibited in some institutions when Black women professionals aspire to and achieve doctorates in order to engage in less teaching and to pursue more research opportunities or achieve administrative/leadership roles—a challenge to competence invisibility from among our colleagues.

The assumption mindset can ignore competence at all levels of academe, and it can suggest that institutional history has no place in the future of an institution. As we become members of these PWIs, the assumption mindset plays a role that easily sets up in-group/out-group stratifications on campus. In her interviews, Margaret Morganroth Gullette discusses how, in the name of being inclusive with budgetary demands as a guide, the in-group can be equated with younger people and innovative ideas versus the current out-group equated with people who are older and more experienced but considered to have fewer creative ideas. The bottom line, however, may depend on how the institution evaluates the cost-effectiveness of its progress in relation to "selective ageist constructs" (Johnson 70). This can be power dominance by positioning.

Martin and Vaughn, in their article "Cultural Competence: The Nuts & Bolts of Diversity & Inclusion" refer to the four stages of the cultural competence development model, which gives insight into the divergent treatment, priority, and attention institutions give to campus diversity programming and initiatives. The stages with their features are:

- the Conventional Stage: very ethnocentric; intolerant and myopic worldviews; blinders to difference and unaware of bias
- the Defensive Stage: bias aware, but go along to get along; anti-affirmative action; tolerance of difference is practiced as protection by law
- the Ambivalent Stage: bias awareness present; supports individual differences, but denies self or organization/institution is biased; and
- the Inclusive Stage: accepts the multicultural nature of human interactions and respects difference, and uses best practices for cultural competence; here allyship is HC at work on a campus.

This leads, then, to some conclusions about the role Black professional women in higher education play in reimagining leadership in academia. I suggest that key points to consider might well be more about what we bring to the professoriate—to classrooms, committees, and boardrooms. Fostering diversity of thought, organization, and strategic outcomes come to mind along with promoting a deep sense of commitment to the tasks both during our time in the classrooms and in positions of empowerment through advancement in leadership positions; tolerance for stress under pressure that comes with the intention of becoming an integral part of any PWI of higher learning; and our often underestimated capability to develop and execute experiential outreach. It is essential to ponder some key steps on those ledges of the glass cliffs as we strategize how best to use our mindsets to navigate the pathways. I believe Black women must:

- know the mountain they're about to climb and the glass cliff onto which they are stepping!
- expect there will be mindsets of various kinds sprinkled or cluttering those ledges up the glass cliff along the way!
- learn to anticipate the narrowed ledges on which they land, very often alone, but be sure-footed!
- be certain not to discount the importance of allyship along the climb, but be intentional in going about it! (Mitchell, "Who's Willing to Walk")
- decide how much of themselves they wish to share and with whom! (Ortiz et al.)
- always maintain integrity and demand respect!
- remember that real competence exudes confidence, and YOU must always know yours!
- Then, Go For It!

All aspiring educational professionals deserve to benefit from what Black women academics bring to higher education. They need to see us in their classrooms as well as in places of more visible campus priority where we can better advocate for their empowered advancement and future global successes.

WORKS CITED

Acker, Joan. "Inequality Regimes: Gender, Class, and Race in Organizations." *Gender and Society*, vol. 20, no. 4, Aug. 2006, pp. 441–64.

American Council on the Teaching of Foreign Languages. *Standards for Foreign Language Learning: Preparing for the 21st Century*. National Standards in Foreign Language Education Project, 1996, ED394279.

Brislin, Richard, and Tomoko Yoshida. *Intercultural Communication Training. An Introduction.* Sage Publications, 1994. Communicating Effectively in Multicultural Contexts 2.

Cushner, Kenneth, and Richard Brislin. *Intercultural Interactions. A Practical Guide.* Sage Publications, 1995. Crosscultural Research and Methodology 9.

Gottfredson, Ryan. "Mindset Differences Across Ethnicities." *Ryan Gottfredson*, 21 June 2021, https://ryangottfredson.com/blog/2021/06/21/mindset-differences-across-ethnicities.

Griffith, Daniel. "What to Do When You Find Yourself in the Out-Group." *Higher Ed Jobs*, 13 Nov. 2019, https://www.higheredjobs.com/articles/article Display.cfm?ID=2078.

Gullette, Margaret Morgenroth. "The Monument and the Wrecking Crew: Ageism in the Academy." *Academe*, vol. 104, no. 3, May–June 2018, pp. 10–15. *American Association of University Professors*, https://www.aaup.org/article/monument-and-wrecking-crew.

Harushimana, Immaculèe, et al., editors. *Reprocessing Race, Language and Ability. African-Born Educators and Students in Transnational America.* Peter Lang, 2013. The Black Studies and Critical Thinking Series 42.

Hofstede, Geert. "Motivation, Leadership, and Organization: Do American Theories Apply Abroad?" *Organizational Dynamics*, vol. 9, no. 1, Summer 1980. *Science Direct*, https://doi.org/10.1016/0090-2616(80)90013-3.

Jack, Zachary M. "Let's Retire Ageism in Academe." *Diverse: Issues in Higher Education*, 24 June 2019. *Diverse*, https://www.diverseeducation.com/faculty-staff/article/15104939/lets-retire-ageism-in-academe.

Johnson, Peggy. "Through a Glass, Darkly: The Hidden Injury of Ageism in the Academy." *Academic Labor: Research and Artistry*, vol. 5, 2021. *Cal Poly Humboldt Digital Commons*, https://digitalcommons.humboldt.edu/alra/vol5/iss1/5.

Martin, Mercedes, and Billy Vaughn. "Cultural Competence: The Nuts & Bolts of Diversity & Inclusion." *Diversity Officer Magazine: Promoting*

Expertise, Research and Credentials, 14 Oct. 2017, https://diversityofficerma-gazine.com/cultural-competence/cultural-competence-the-nuts-bolts-of -diversity-inclusion-2/.

Mitchell, Janice D. M. *Multicultural Studies: Crosscultural Awareness in the Pluralistic (Urban) Classroom. A Guide for Future Teachers of the Hearing-Impaired and Others. Department of Education Foundations and Research*. Gallaudet College, 1982.

———*The Relationship of Foreign Language Training to the Written Grammar and Written English of Deaf College Students and The Implications for Teaching the Written Grammars of Spoken Languages to the Postsecondary Hearing Impaired*. 1981. University of Southern California, EdD dissertation.

———"Who's Willing to Walk the Edge with Me? Calling All Allies!" *Institute for Diversity Trainers Resource Manual*. Edited by Cris C. Cullinan et al. The 16th Annual National Conference on Race and Ethnicity in American Higher Education. National Conference on Race and Ethnicity in Higher Education, 2003.

Mitchell, Janice D. M., and Carolyn McCaskill. *Multiple Perspectives: Cultural Heritage and Its Implication on Identity*. General Studies Requirement 211 with a Service Learning Component. From the course syllabus.

Mitchell, Janice D. M., and Kamakshi P. Murti. *Fostering and Promoting Inclusion: A Training Manual for Achieving Excellence in Written and Oral Communication for Successful Student Leadership*. 5 Aug. 2021.

Mthethwa-Sommers, Shirley. *Teaching Against Defensive Moves: A Case Study on the Impact of Teacher Racial Identity on Learning*. 10 Apr. 2013, SSRN, https://ssrn.com/abstract=2247821.

Ortiz, Angelica Paz, et al. "Positionality in Teaching: Implications for Advocacy Social Justice." *The Journal of General Education*, vol. 67, no. 1–2, 2018, pp. 109–21. *Scholarly Publishing Collective*, https://doi.org/10.5325 /jgeneeduc.67.1-2.0109.

Reed-Danahay, Deborah. "Bourdieu and Critical Autoethnography: Implications for Research, Writing and Teaching." *International Journal of Multicultural Education*, vol. 19, no. 1, 2017, pp.144–54.

Samovar, Larry A., and Richard E. Porter. *Intercultural Communication: A Reader*. Wadsworth, 1994.

Weick, Karl E. *Sensemaking in Organizations. Foundations for Organizational Science*. Vol. 3, Sage, 1995.

Winters, Mary-Frances. "Creating Brave, Psychologically Safe Spaces." *Inclusive Conversations. Fostering Equity, Empathy, and Belonging across Differences*. Berrett-Koehler, 2020.

FROM THE CHRYSALIS TO THE LONG GREEN TABLE

Closing Thoughts

OLGA M. WELCH

E
ndings always bring challenges. For us, this volume is no different. Even as we prepared our introduction and opening chapter
and showcased the subsequent authors' perspectives, we found
ourselves reflecting on concluding thoughts with which we wanted to
leave our readers. This book has focused deliberately on the experiences
of Black women leaders in higher education because the literature still
contains relatively little scholarship from or about these administrators
in the academy. In our introduction, we used as a metaphor for these
women the "chrysalis" that produces and also strengthens the butterfly
that emerges. Whether abutting the "glass ceiling" or scaling the "glass
cliff," they have encountered traditional as well as particularly unique experiences that require exploration and scholarly interrogation.

For us, part of that interrogation has involved moving beyond the literature on educational administration and policy studies in higher education to examinations of leadership theories and practices in business,
the military, and history, among other disciplines. The more we have ex-
plored, the more intrigued we have become with the conundrum within
an enigma that effective leadership represents in a variety of contexts.
Thus, we wanted to offer our readers some closing ideas for reflection
and thought.

We begin with a question posed by Admiral Wiliam H. McRaven, US Navy (Retired), in his 2023 book, *The Wisdom of the Bullfrog: Leadership Made Simple (But Not Easy)*. It is the question that guided his decision-making process, as a leader, throughout his military career. Admiral McRaven notes: "Whenever I had a difficult decision to make, I would ask myself, 'Can you stand before the long, green table?'"

> Since WWII, the conference tables used in military boardrooms had been constructed of long, narrow pieces of furniture covered in green felt. Whenever a formal proceeding took place that required multiple officers to adjudicate an issue, the officers would gather around the table. The point of the saying was simple. If you couldn't make a good case to the officers sitting around the long green table, then you should reconsider your actions. It is one of the most fundamental questions leaders must ask themselves . . . and the old saying helped me remember what steps to take. (iv)

As we conclude this volume, we pose the same question to ourselves and to present and future leaders who may read it. The chrysalis that produces the butterfly requires struggle. Similarly, the crucible of leadership requires constant introspection and retrospection—the willingness to pose new questions and engage in sometimes painful reexaminations of leadership missteps occasioned sometimes by the self-assurance of self-serving hubris and the unwillingness to unflinchingly "stand before the long green table" to reconsider the actions taken.

McRaven asserts that "leadership is never easy. Everything in leadership is simple, it's just that the simplest things are difficult" (xii). Throughout this volume, our contributors have offered their own maxims and perspectives as Black female leaders in the academy. Yet while not difficult to express, they are infinitely more complicated to enact in practice. Why? Because again, as McRaven contends, "we are humans and each of us has our foibles, our weaknesses, our shortfalls that can affect how we lead" (xiiv). However, given that reality, as difficult as leadership is, it is *not* complicated. It *is* both science and art—that is, "getting the job done" but also inspiring the women and men who make that possible while simultaneously maintaining or advancing the reputation of your institution. Thus, explaining your actions, first to yourself and then to others—standing before the long green table—becomes an introspective and retrospective journey of "adult learning" (xiiv). Bennis references Plato, who observed that "learning is basically recovery or recollection" (x). He notes that in the case of leadership, what we need to know gets lost in what we are *told* we should know. Thus, real learning is a matter of remembering what is important, not just what we are told is important. We would argue that Black female leaders already know what they need to know at some level; it is recovering that basic knowledge and confidence within challenging administrative contexts that may be daunting.

One thing Black women leaders know from their history and the legacy from which they learned is that a more dangerous and unpredictable world makes the need for leadership in every organization and every institution more pressing than ever. The chrysalis produces the butterfly and, as such, serves as a crucible, a rite of passage, in which transformative strength emerges. What then, are the essential competencies, in addition to the qualities described by our contributors, that a Black woman leader must possess? Bennis offers four essential competencies that effective leaders must possess. However, he maintains that the most important of these is adaptive capacity. Adaptive capacity is what allows a leader to respond quickly and intelligently to relentless change. Adaptive capacity allows leaders to act, and to evaluate the results of their actions. Adaptive capacity involves hardiness and creativity, the ability to seize opportunities, including the ability to find and somehow woo great mentors, to spot the handful of people who can make all the difference in one's life and get them on your side (x).

The history of slavery in America and its aftermath of Jim Crow segregation and the quest for civil rights represent the basic knowledge that Black women leaders bring to the academy. They also bring the authenticity of "character." Bennis argues that timeless leadership is always about character. We assert that one cannot conquer glass cliffs without it. Emerging from the chrysalis in order to stand confidently before "the green table" requires wisdom. Socrates is credited with observing that the beginning of wisdom is a recognition of one's own ignorance. We maintain that such recognition requires constant reflection and introspection, a journey of self-discovery that allows the Black woman leader not just to burnish her credentials but also to acknowledge her own ignorance as she develops and cultivates wisdom.

WORKS CITED

Bennis, Warren. *On Becoming a Leader*. 4th ed., Basic Books, 2009.
McRaven, William H. *Leadership Made Simple (But Not Easy)*. Grand Central Publishing, 2023.

AFTERWORD

"They Wouldn't Let Us Lead..."

CAROL CAMP YEAKEY

"You've got to be twice as good to get half as far."
—MICHELLE OBAMA, SPEECH AT THE 2024 DEMOCRATIC
NATIONAL CONVENTION

This volume, *Black Women Leading in Higher Education*, could not come at a more auspicious time. We have witnessed recent retrenchment in historic gains for African Americans and other marginalized groups, long thought cemented, but now being erased. Supreme Court reversals and bans from affirmative action to diversity and inclusion, to book censorship, to a growing intolerance of anything and anyone that does not embrace the hegemony and paternalism of white male society is at risk. The chapters in this volume bear witness to the pain, sacrifice, and talents of not only Black women contributors, but also their mentors and the shoulders of so many women on which they have stood. Suffering from that pernicious intersectional duality of race and gender, African American women, as this volume reminds us, have never ceased to climb, never failed to rise to the occasion of leadership challenges, no matter the obstacles in front of them. While we see ourselves in these women, what we do not see are their sacrifices, their tears, their pains, and the feelings of loneliness and isolation that being in leadership positions brings forth. We know the names of our more famous sisters who saw the top and reached for it, but the ceiling was snatched from their grasp, not due to their inadequacies, but due to the inadequacies of others. We know the recent victims from among those who dared to lead, most notably, Kamala Harris, Claudine Gay, Anita Hill, Antoinette Bonnie Candia-Bailey (who died by suicide), Shirley Chisholm, Barbara Ann Sizemore, Rosa Parks, Daisy Bates, Fannie Lou Hamer, Harriet Tubman, Sojourner Truth, Ida B. Wells, Anna Julia Cooper (Moody-Turner), among many others who have yet to be fully appreciated or justly rewarded. We give tribute to them by saying their names. We dare not forget the less well-known talented Black women who possessed every skill set required for leadership, but who stood in the background, in support of others, most often males who were far less talented. We, women of color, do not have the luxury of what Michelle Obama calls "failing forward and having the affirmative action of generational wealth." When Black women have the luxury of failure, and then being rewarded with positions of high leadership and unparalleled success as though failure has never occurred, perhaps then we will have achieved true equality with white society.

We Black women know the story too well:

- being awarded a leadership position, yet being held to a different and higher standard than white men and women, and leaders of other racial identities
- suffering from the lack of tangible and intangible supports to which white peers have access
- being offered leadership positions at times of great change, scrutiny, or tumult
- being excluded from the informal social networks that undergird systemic supports, rewards, and strategic information
- undergoing the "glass cliff effect," which speaks to the lack of higher-level administrative supports to challenge well-known, documented, systemic cultures that foster discrimination and undermine inequity
- carrying the psychological and emotional toll, often called "the

Black tax," of not just being Black, but being a Black woman, where one's authority, intelligence, credibility and self-worth are questioned

- receiving less tangible remuneration and reward for performing the same tasks as white peers in similar leadership positions.

We live in a time of growing division between the haves and have-nots, as well as growing polarization in not only our country but across the globe. Recent events reveal that decency, integrity, and equal justice before the law serve the few, not the many. Nevertheless, I have tremendous hope in the future. As Dr. Martin Luther King, Jr., reminds us, "[T]he arc of the moral universe is long, but it bends toward justice." The contributors to this volume recognize the enduring nature of social struggle in the pursuit of fairness and justice for all. Our historic journeys and struggles as African Americans have never been immediate, or effortless, or painless, but have spanned generations and centuries. Simply put, we have gone too far, endured too much, suffered too long, to give up our pursuit of fairness and our just rewards in the workplace, and in broader society.

WORKS CITED

King, Jr., Martin Luther. "Remaining Awake Through a Great Revolution." Speech at the Washington National Cathedral, D.C., 31 Mar. 1968, https://www.seemeonline.com/history/mlk-jr-awake.html.

Moody-Turner, Shirley. "How the Black Female Head of a Top D.C. School was 'Punished for Leading.'" *Washington Post*, 19 Mar. 2024, https://www.washingtonpost.com/opinions/2024/03/19/anna-julia-cooper-dc-education-dunbar.

Obama, Michelle. "Speech at the 2024 Democratic National Convention." *Time*, 21 Aug. 2024, https://time.com/7013289/michelle-obama-2024-dnc-speech-full-transcript/.

INDEX

CONTRIBUTORS

Wanda J. Blanchett, PhD, Distinguished Professor, Former Dean of the Graduate School of Education and Special Advisor to the Chancellor for Academic Affairs and Equity, and Interim Provost and Executive Vice Chancellor for Academic Affairs, Rutgers University-New Brunswick

Wanda Blanchett's research focuses on educational inequities, including urban teacher preparation; issues of race, class, culture, and gender; disproportionate representation of students of color in special education; issues of sexuality for students with disabilities; and transitioning into higher education academic leadership. She is a past chair of the American Association for Colleges of Teacher Education (AACTE) Board of Directors and Global Diversity Committee, and a past member of the AERA/OIA Executive Committee, and elected treasurer for the Council for Academic Deans from Research Education Institutions (CADREI) Executive Committee.

Tam'ra-Kay Francis, PhD, Research Faculty, College of Engineering, University of Washington

Tam'ra-Kay Francis is an educator with over twenty years of experience working with programs designed to provide holistic support for minoritized students. Her two-word mantra, "beyond category," is the center of her work, which examines STEM identity development as part of social and cultural contexts both within disciplines and in transdisciplinary environments. A fierce advocate for equity and access, her current efforts at the University of Washington engage both faculty and students in the evaluation of curricular and co-curricular innovations in STEM. She was recently named a "rising star" on a list of one thousand inspiring Black scientists in America.

Carolyn R. Hodges, PhD, Professor Emerita of German Studies; Vice Provost and Dean Emerita of the Graduate School, University of Tennessee, Knoxville

Carolyn R. Hodges was a professor of German in the Department of World Languages and Cultures at the University of Tennessee. She served as head of that department, as associate dean for Academic Personnel in the College of Arts and Sciences, and for nine years as vice provost and dean of the Graduate School, after which she chaired the Africana Studies Program for three years. She was elected president of the Southern Comparative Literature Association (SCLA), is a board member of the Georgiana Simpson Society for German Diaspora Studies, and served on regional and national boards for graduate education and German Studies. Her publications focus on perspectives in Black German literature, comparative literature, and leadership. She is a member of the Board of Trustees for Arcadia University, Glenside, PA.

She and the volume coeditor, Olga Welch, are partners in Welch and Hodges, LLC, Higher Education Consultants and Leadership Training.

Janice D. M. Mitchell, EdD, Certified Diversity Professional, Professor Emerita, Gallaudet University

Janice Mitchell's teaching and research span many years of pioneering work on language acquisition of deaf students learning foreign languages and English. She created multiple courses across the curriculum and programming in Multicultural Studies for future teachers; worked prominently in urban settings with Teaching English to Speakers of Other Languages (TESOL); used various methods in addition to sign language to teach German and English for General Studies students, language majors, and language minors; and developed courses and trained teachers in direct and indirect service learning techniques and study abroad best practices. She has also served as a department head at Gallaudet, faculty vice president, and the executive director of the Fulbright German-American Cultural Exchange Program. As a certified diversity professional, she conducts training workshops and institutes, and consults on cross-cultural aspects of diversity, equity, and inclusion for effective leadership.

Stephanie J. Rowley, PhD, Dean and William R. Kenan, Jr. Professor of Education, School of Education and Human Development, University of Virginia

Stephanie Rowley's research explores how parents' attitudes toward race and gender and their own social experiences influence their children's motivation and identity in school. She is currently conducting a longitudinal study of African American parents' beliefs about STEM disciplines and how those beliefs affect middle school youth. Her work has been funded by the National Science Foundation. Prior to joining the University of Virginia, Dr. Rowley served as provost, dean, and vice president for academic affairs at Teachers College, Columbia University. Before that, she spent nineteen years as a professor and administrator, including associate vice president for research, at the University of Michigan.

Olga M. Welch, EdD, Professor and Dean Emerita

Olga M. Welch served for a decade as dean of the School of Education at Duquesne University. Previously she had been a professor in the Department of Theory and Practice in Teacher Education at the University of Tennessee. She was appointed interim head of the Educational Administration and Policy Studies Department and head of the Counseling, Deafness and Human Services Department. She has published widely on executive mentoring, social justice, equity, and diversity, including an edited volume, *Turnaround Leadership: Deans of Color as Change Agents* (Peter Lang, 2012). She has been a reviewer for the United States Department of Education and chaired several regional and national advisory boards in education. She was a member of the US Department of Health's African American Health Care Congress, the

African American Prenatal Issues Task Force, and is an inaugural fellow for the Initiative on Race, Research, and Justice at Vanderbilt University.

She and the volume coeditor, Carolyn Hodges, are partners in Welch and Hodges, LLC, Higher Education Consultants and Leadership Training.

Carol Camp Yeakey, PhD, Marshall S. Snow Professor of Arts & Sciences and Professor of Public Health in the School of Public Health at Washington University in St. Louis

Carol Camp Yeakey is the Marshall S. Snow Professor of Arts & Sciences and founding director of the interdisciplinary program in Urban Studies and its Center on Urban Research and Public Policy at Washington University in St. Louis. She holds appointments as professor of Education, of American Culture Studies, of Urban Studies, and of Public Policy and is a faculty scholar in the Institute for Public Health and Professor of Public Health in the School of Public Health. Yeakey was elected a member of the National Academy of Education in 2016, received the Distinguished Career Contribution to Research Award by the American Education Research Association (AERA) in 2012, and was awarded an American Council on Education (ACE) Fellowship for higher education leadership development in 2004.